YOUNG GUNS

——————— ★ ———————

A NEW GENERATION

of

CONSERVATIVE LEADERS

ERIC CANTOR,
PAUL RYAN,
and KEVIN McCARTHY

Threshold Editions
New York   London   Toronto   Sydney

Threshold Editions
A Division of Simon & Schuster, Inc.
1230 Avenue of the Americas
New York, NY 10020

First Threshold Editions trade paperback edition September 2010

THRESHOLD EDITIONS and colophon are trademarks of Simon & Schuster, Inc.

For information about special discounts for bulk purchases, please contact Simon & Schuster Special Sales at 1-866-506-1949 or business@simonandschuster.com.

The Simon & Schuster Speakers Bureau can bring authors to your live event. For more information or to book an event contact the Simon & Schuster Speakers Bureau at 1-866-248-3049 or visit our website at www.simonspeakers.com.

Designed by Bill Ruoto

Manufactured in the United States of America

10 9 8 7 6 5 4 3 2 1

Library of Congress Cataloging-in-Publication Data
Cantor, Eric.
    Young guns : a new generation of conservative leaders / by Eric Cantor, Paul Ryan, and Kevin McCarthy. — Threshold editions.
        p. cm.
        1. Conservatives—United States.   2. Conservatism—United States.
3. United States—Politics and government—1989–   I. Ryan, Paul.
II. McCarthy, Kevin.   III. Title.
    JC573.2.U6C36 2010
    320.520973—dc22   2010018512

ISBN 978-1-4516-0734-5
ISBN 978-1-4516-0735-2 (ebook)

Table of Contents

——— ★ ———

FOREWORD *by Fred Barnes* . . . . *vii*

MEET THE YOUNG GUNS:
A ROUNDTABLE DISCUSSION · *1*

PART 1 · ERIC CANTOR

1   *A Party on the Bridge to Nowhere* *19*

2   *A Year of Living Dangerously* *39*

3   *A Better Way* *67*

Table of Contents

PART 2 · PAUL RYAN

4   *Health-Care Reform and the* *91*
     New Way in Washington

5   *The Tipping Point* *109*

6   *A Roadmap for America's Future* *125*

PART 3 · KEVIN McCARTHY

7   *The Politics of Re-Earning Trust* *141*

8   *Young Guns* *155*

9   *A Commitment to America* *177*

     Appendix A *193*

     Appendix B *195*

     Acknowledgments *197*

     Index *199*

Foreword

———— ★ ————

When they came together in 2007, Eric Cantor, Paul Ryan, and Kevin McCarthy didn't seem to be a natural fit. They were young, conservative Republican members of the House of Representatives, but elected at different times, from distant regions of the country, and their political skills were anything but similar. Yet having joined forces as leaders of Young Guns, they now represent the Republican future in Congress.

Cantor was elected from Richmond and its suburbs in Virginia in 2000 and two years later was already on the leadership track. He'd been spotted by then House Republican whip Roy Blunt and chosen as chief deputy whip. In 1998 at age twenty-eight, Ryan won a House seat from the southern tier of Wisconsin. By 2004, he'd emerged as the congressman who knew more about the federal budget, taxes, entitlements, and health care than anyone else in Washington and understood the need for radical measures to reform them. McCarthy was elected in 2006 from an agricultural and oil-producing district in the San Joaquin Valley in California. Even before he arrived on Capitol Hill, he had campaigned for many of his Republican colleagues and was familiar with most of the others. In 2008, Cantor tapped McCarthy as his chief deputy whip.

What prompted Cantor, Ryan, and McCarthy to come together was a story in *The Weekly Standard* (with separate profiles on each of them). They appeared on the cover in a photo taken on a Capitol balcony overlooking the Mall. They were all smiles. They knew each other as members of the embattled Republican caucus that had lost control of the House in the disastrous 2006 mid-term election. But they hadn't realized their individual skills were remarkably complementary: Cantor the leader, Ryan the thinker, McCarthy the strategist. Some of us at *The Weekly Standard* had noticed this. Thus the cover story.

In a sense, their alliance and the creation of Young Guns was a revolt against the older, established Republican leaders in the House. The party establishment was dedicated to protecting incumbents at all cost. With money, manpower, and advice, Young Guns supports challengers, many in races that otherwise might be ignored by the national party. Young Guns is partial to young, reform-minded Republicans. It is eager to erase the image of congressional Republicans as big spenders preoccupied with assuring their own reelection. In short, Cantor, Ryan, and McCarthy would like to fill the ranks of House Republicans with members, like themselves, committed to policies and legislation infused with the principles of limited government, free markets, and individual freedom. Young Guns is not for "me-too" Republicans, those comfortable with a scaled-back version of the Democratic agenda.

Cantor had followed the advice of his predecessor from the Richmond district and political mentor, Tom Bliley. Stay off the Commerce Committee or you'll be written off as tobacco's man in Washington, Bliley told him. It would be a liability if he sought a spot in the House leadership. Instead, with a law degree and a background in his family's real estate management firm, Cantor angled to be on the tax-writing (or tax cutting) Ways and Means Committee. So when Blunt called him in 2002, he expected to be offered a seat on Ways and Means. But Blunt had noticed his leadership attributes: energetic, respected by colleagues, his conservatism tempered by a streak of caution. And Blunt and his aides weren't shy about touting Cantor's performance as deputy whip.

In his dozen years in Congress, Ryan has managed to avoid being tied down by whatever is the issue of the day. This is perhaps the hardest thing for a member of Congress to do, especially an ambitious backbencher. But Ryan's models when he first came to Washington as a staffer were Jack Kemp and Bill Bennett—Republican thinkers. He worked for Kemp and Bennett and later for Sen. Sam

Brownback (when I met him), thinking all the time about everything that Washington touches. Now he's the most influential Republican thinker in Congress. His magnum opus is called A Roadmap for America's Future. It's a sweeping plan to reform the way Washington works.

I met McCarthy in 2004 when he was the Republican leader in the lower house of the California legislature. At a Washington dinner just before President Bush's second inauguration, my friend Jim Brulte introduced McCarthy as the California Republican with the greatest future. Brulte, then Republican leader in the state Senate, was right. Besides being Cantor's top deputy, McCarthy is an expert on how to win House races. He dropped by my office several months after the Republican debacle in 2006. He'd just been elected to his first term. He was already working on a strategy for political recovery. In 2010, he led the effort to recruit electable Republican House candidates. McCarthy's favorites? Candidates fresh to politics and bursting with enthusiasm about reforming Washington.

The future of Young Guns and its three honchos is unquestionably bright. I'm convinced Eric Cantor will be speaker or majority leader the next time Republicans control the House. When that happens, Paul Ryan will be chairman of the House Budget Committee and will be in line to become chairman of the House Ways and Means Committee. The first order of business as chairman of House Ways and Means will be fundamental tax and entitlement reform. The second order of business will be more reform.

As for McCarthy, he'll be right behind Cantor in the leadership, either as majority leader or whip—and someday, if Cantor steps aside, even House Speaker. All the while, he'll be fixated on how to win more elections, more often. In short, Young Guns is not only here to stay, but to succeed.

Fred Barnes
April, 2010

———— ★ ————

MEET THE YOUNG GUNS:

A ROUNDTABLE

DISCUSSION

————— ★ —————

*O*n March 11, 2010, House Republicans agreed to a one-year moratorium on earmarks—or, as they are referred to informally—sweetheart deals. A few hours later, Congressmen Eric Cantor of Virginia, Paul Ryan of Wisconsin, and Kevin McCarthy of California gathered around Diet Cokes and bottled water to discuss this milestone and how it fits into their vision of change in Washington.

PR: We've been like Sisyphus on this thing. We've been pulling this earmark moratorium rock up the hill only to be rolled over with it by the people who like earmarks. We've been working on this thing for five years.

EC: I think enough members finally realized that

the level of frustration among the public is at such a fever pitch right now that we had no choice. We had to say enough is enough.

PR: Yeah, this was culture change for our conference [the House Republicans]. And it just shows that our conference is beginning to acknowledge reality, acknowledge where the people are.

KM: Part of this stems from the town hall meetings. They've changed people's minds. If you've been out there lately, you know that the public is screaming for this. And there's also the fact that we're coming off a month in which we hit $200 billion, just for this month, in the deficit.

EC: I think being in the extreme minority is what it took for us to have the dose of contrition necessary to do this. But I also think you're seeing now an administration and a congressional leadership in Nancy Pelosi that is so extreme in ignoring the public. We see it and feel it when we go home. People are so upset. Earmarks are such a symbol of the problem in Washington. We know the moratorium doesn't fix the problem but it certainly is the beginning. It's a recognition that we need to change the culture.

KM: On the flight in this week, it just happened that sitting next to me was Gary Hart. We were having a kind of generational talk about Washington. And one of the things he pointed out that was wrong with Washington was earmarks. He said Republicans and Democrats had both been poisoned by earmarks.

PR: The way I see what happened with this earmark moratorium is we have finally begun to cleanse ourselves of the corruption that occurred when Republicans were in the majority. I was a staffer here during the mid-1990s after the Contract with America. That was an incredible Congress of people from a cross section of America. Doctors, small businesspeople, insurance brokers, farmers—people from all across America. We had people who really believed in ideas and principles. And then slowly but surely as the conference matured, they started to recruit career politicians as opposed to citizen legislators. They brought in more machine-like people. And I think our leadership changed and adopted the position that, well, we beat the Democrats' machine, now it's time to create a Republican machine to keep us in the majority. And out of that came this earmark culture.

KM: Our recruits this time are like 1994. We've got new blood coming in here. New recruits and reinforcements to get us back to our roots as a party, back to reclaiming the American idea and stopping the careerism.

EC: We really are beginning to feel like we're on offense now. We lost our way when we were in the majority. We stopped playing offense. We lost our sense of what we were here for. It was almost as if the institution overcame us and became the priority. Now, being in the deep minority we've gained a better sense of where we need to take this country and where we need to lead. It starts with recognizing that the people expect a certain level of conduct and behavior and the people expect a certain level of humility out of their government, in contrast to the arrogance they see coming out of the majority today.

PR: And we also have to declare our principles. They are the nation's founding principles. And then we have to show how we are going to apply them to the problems of the day. And show how we will use these principles to guide our actions in a very transparent and clear way. I think what happened to the Republicans before was we had a majority of people who came here to do something and we atrophied into a majority of people who came here to be something.

KM: And we lost our ideas along the way.

PR: Yeah, we lost ideas and we lost our core. Now we're back to being doers again because we're seeing what the Democrats are offering. We're seeing how they want to transform this country into a cradle-to-grave European social welfare state and change the idea of America forever.

KM: There was a group of us at a dinner on the night of the inaugural. We got together because we weren't invited to anything else [laughter]. But instead of drowning our sorrows, we talked about how to rebuild and how to come back to our principles. That was a turning point.

EC: And at the same time, Democrats were assuming that they had this mandate. They assumed that there had been an ideological shift in this country toward big government and that they had a license to change this country. But this country is not about transformational change because it is firmly rooted in the first principles of our nation. Nobody wants to mess with these founding principles. But Democrats somehow convinced themselves that now was the time for America to enter the new world order; now was the time for us to become more European. And they launched an effort that has become very frightening for the American people.

PR: They shocked the American people. They shocked us. They certainly shocked me. I wasn't sure what kind of president Obama was going to be. I thought, maybe this guy is going to be a centrist—his rhetoric was centrist. His upbringing and his history didn't suggest he was centrist but his rhetoric did. So I was thinking, well, we'll see. And then—bam!—out of the gates, these people had a hardcore-left agenda. We, along with the American people, were spectators while they took this government very far left, very fast. But what became so unnerving to us and the American people is that they used *our* rhetoric. They used the rhetoric of freedom and choice and opportunity to sell an inherently statist agenda; to sell an agenda that was completely the opposite of its rhetoric. And people started to realize that they were trying to transform the country using the rhetoric of the Right to push through the substance of the Left.

KM: It was the stimulus bill that woke us up. Remember, the president was still at 70 percent approval. He comes into our caucus and says he's going to work with us on a bill. Then we walk out and Speaker Pelosi introduces a bill without our input.

EC: It became a very defining moment for this conference, that stimulus bill.

PR: Very much so.

KM: Remember the hours we spent sitting in Eric's conference room drafting the alternative to the stimulus? We drafted an alternative that was better, that created twice the jobs for half the money. I think that's when we got our mojo back.

PR: And then as the year went on, if you listened to the new majority it was actually pretty clear what their intentions were. I remember being up until midnight one night debating the health-care bill in early November [2009]. Emotions were running very high. Everyone was coming to the floor and really speaking their mind. And I sat there and watched liberal dinosaur after liberal dinosaur—people who have been in Congress longer than I've been living or since I was in the first or second grade—and they all basically said the same thing, which really opened my eyes. They said, "This is finally our opportunity to bring about the completion of the progressive agenda." One of them said this was the "third wave of progressivism. There was the New Deal, the Great Society, and now we are completing the vision of transforming America into what it needs to be." And what that means is turning the Constitution on its head, forgetting about the idea of equal opportunity.

EC: It became about them. It became about their sense of why they were here and their desire to win.

PR: And it became about the destiny they had charted for themselves, which, I think, helped us reach our own sense of destiny.

EC: And it was so anathema to what the American people were thinking at the time or wanted for this country. That's what the country saw. They saw that the powers in charge here are ignorant of what the people want and frankly arrogant about it. And it became more about their need to win. Look at the health-care debate. It's tough for them to get their minds around the fact that the people don't want this country transformed the way they want it. They just believe that, number one, the means justify the ends. And number two, that this country needs to become more like a social democracy.

KM: That government knows better.

PR: It's completely antithetical to what this country is about.

EC: They really believe there is an inherent unfairness in the free market and that they need to be the ones to intervene to right the wrongs of the markets and of the big bad world of business. They believe that some people make too much money, others don't. They believe they're here to accomplish equal outcomes, not equal opportunity.

KM: Look at President Obama. Who has been close to him? Trial lawyers, unions, community organizers. All three are redistributers of wealth, not creators of wealth. So in his mind he's always thought, "I need to redistribute wealth. I don't need to worry about creating wealth, because that just always happens."

PR: It's a fundamental misunderstanding of

human nature and of the concepts of liberty, freedom, and self-determination. It's a fundamental misunderstanding of economics. He believes that the pie is fixed and that he needs to more equitably divide up the slices.

KM: He doesn't believe in growing the pie.

PR: They're making a political calculation. Right now, we are a right-of-center country. But if they can create the newest and biggest entitlement we've ever had they can take us past the tipping point, after which more people are takers rather than makers—more people are living off the state than are living independent of it. I believe they think the orientation of the country will turn and become a left-of-center country. This is an investment in their future. They're going to take some short-term losses but they will come back because they are completing the vision they have for this country.

KM: They think if they make government so large and the debt so big it will be impossible to reverse it.

PR: The American government, in their minds, isn't nearly as big as it ought to be compared to our Western European counterparts. We're historically at 20 percent of GDP. They think we ought to go to 30 percent of GDP for the federal government. You add in state and local government and you're at 50 percent of GDP and that's where Europe is.

EC: This time in the minority has given us all a chance to remember why we came here. It's given us the chance—especially in comparison with what the Democrats are doing—to see what has worked in this country, which is entrepreneurship, free markets, and a level playing field. We need to refocus our party toward the future and the young people. It's up to us to provide them with more opportunity. I hear it again and again when I go home. Right now kids are getting out of college and they're not finding jobs. So if we reclaim the majority in November, we must, first of all, tell the public what they can expect from us. And we also have to realize that this isn't going to be a one- or two-year process. We have got to rebuild the public's trust through taking concrete steps to get our fiscal house in order. We have to show that we get it. Clearly the other side has demonstrated that they don't get where the public is. We've got to reconnect and inspire people.

PR: The American people still love the American idea. And the American idea is at risk today. So in this election and in the 2012 election we have to give the American people a very clear agenda based upon our actions and our principles. We have to give them a very clear choice.

KM: That's why I think the time is right. You value things the most when you lose them. Who would have thought America could be going the way it's going now? With government taking over businesses? With government taking over health care? We've always believed in freedom as a country but now we're starting to understand that we have to fight for it.

PR: If we get this majority, we have to build on it. We have to go to the American people with an agreement. We've got to show how we can restore this country's greatness by reasserting and reapplying its principles.

EC: What we have to do is lay out an agenda toward which we can lead the people and they'll come along and back us. People get that there is unsustainable spending going on; that we're spending money we don't have right now. But I don't think most people wake up in the morning and think about our entitlement programs crashing. We have to be able to connect that circumstance with their everyday lives. That has to be the impetus for us to begin to devolve power back to the states.

KM: It's unshackling the grip that Washington has on so much of our lives.

EC: Right, but we're going to have to be able to go to the people and demonstrate how that helps them. Like in the area of education. Joe Pitts [R-PA] has a program he's worked on for years that's all about dollars in the schools and dollars in the classrooms, not dollars to the unions and the bureaucracy. We have to go to parents and say we are about letting the local schools get more dollars and that means don't let the dollars be trapped here in Washington. Same thing with transportation.

PR: People think that their country is slipping away from them. They think that their future is not going to be as bright. So they're ready to embrace a reclamation of what made this country great. And if we get back into the majority we cannot fall from this fight. We can't be intimidated. We can't worry about the demagoguery and the negative ads we're going to get.

KM: But you also have to create a system that allows your changes to endure. It goes back to what Eric said about education. The average salary in the Department of Education right down the street here is $103,000. That's the average salary of the employee that works there. Wouldn't that money be better spent in the classroom?

EC: You get a double benefit from ending that. If you're going to keep dollars in the classrooms, not only are you benefiting the kids but you're also reducing the size of Washington, which helps to get rid of the corruption and the cronyism and the self-perpetuating nature of power here.

KM: We have four million more government jobs in America than manufacturing jobs. That is an upside-down model.

PR: That's right. People are getting a glimpse of what this country could become. They know that's not who we are. They know that's not reaching our potential. I think people are ready if we show them a party of leadership and of principle and an agenda that gets it.

KM: It has to be accountable.

PR: We have to give the American people a referendum. We will win this referendum if we have it now. If we wait and delay five or six years we will lose this referendum. The public is way ahead of the political class. They get that things are broken. They get that we're spending their kids' inheritance and mortgaging their future. They are ready to be talked to like adults and not like children. So, when they see the demagoguery that is directed toward people or ideas that are sincere and are real, it doesn't work anymore. The Democrats are going to come at us with their old playbook. They're going to tap into the emotions of fear, anger, and envy. But that's not aspirational. That's not hope and change, and I don't think it's going to work anymore.

EC: There is a test for us though. This country is changing demographically. This country is growing older and we've been in an entitlement mindset for a while. That's what we're going to change. We're going to be about an opportunity future, not an entitlement future. That's why it's important that we go out and make the case to those nearing retirement that they're not going to be denied what they have coming.

PR: But if we act now, it won't be all root canal. This is growth, this is opportunity, this is hope. This is maintaining our commitments to those who are nearing retirement. If we act now, we can honor those commitments. If we don't act, we won't be able to.

PART ONE

——— ★ ———

CONGRESSMAN

ERIC CANTOR

CHAPTER ONE

A Party on the Bridge to Nowhere

———— ★ ————

A Jewish guy from Virginia, an Irish-Catholic from Wisconsin, and a California Baptist walk into Congress. . . .

It sounds like the beginning of an old joke, but we'd like to think it's the start of something new.

Paul, Kevin, and I are, as Bill Murray famously said to his demoralized fellow recruits on graduation day in *Stripes*, "very different people. We're not Watusi. We're not Spartans. We're Americans, with a capital 'A.' " The three of us came to the United States House of Representatives from very different places. No one will ever mistake Janesville, Wisconsin (or Richmond, Virginia, for that matter), for Bakersfield, California. We also come from very different backgrounds. I pray on Saturday with a Southern accent. Paul and Kevin go to church on Sunday and talk to God without dropping their "gs."

What we have in common is our love for this country and the principles that made it great. From our different vantage points, we've seen both parties abandon these principles and lead America down a perilous path. We've seen Republicans who claim to believe in limited government spend the taxpayers' money like teenagers with their parents' credit card. We've seen Democrats who claim to want only government that "works" never pass up an opportunity to make government bigger and more intrusive. We've seen both parties ignore the needs of Americans while they concentrate on doing favors for the special interests that get them reelected, whether it's unions, corporations, or any of the army of lobbyists encamped on Capitol Hill.

Don't get me wrong. We're proud Republicans. We just believe that our party has at times lost sight of the things we believe in, ideas like economic freedom, limited government, the sanctity of life, and putting families first. America needs new leaders with new solutions for the challenges we face. We don't expect *The New York Times* to agree with us, but we believe these leaders and these solutions can't come from the party in control of Washington today. They have to come from the party whose principles are firmly grounded in encouraging private sector job creation, in maximizing individual freedom—whether it's the freedom to choose your own doctor or the freedom to choose the school for your kids—and in giving all Americans the opportunity to build a better future for their children. That party is the party of Lincoln and Reagan; it's the party of Rubio, Jindal, and Daniels.

We believe it's time for Republicans to reconnect with our principles, reinvigorate our message, and show our true face to America. We respect those who came before us, but as far as Paul, Kevin, and I are concerned, America is looking for more than our grandfather's Republican Party. The wonderful irony of America is that it is a dynamic, diverse, and changing country that was founded on timeless, unchanging ideas. We're ready to take our belief in the ideas that have made America great and translate them into the solutions that will make our future even better.

America is ready for a new direction—the country urgently *needs* a new direction—the only question is: who is going to provide it? The people we talk to and hear from everyday have made it clear that they're not in love with either party these days. Republicans controlled Washington from 2001 to 2006. They did some good things but they also did a lot to give conservatism a bad name. Then Democrats took power and their one party rule for the past year and a half has made "liberal" a fighting word. Neither party has addressed a building crisis in America; a crisis of government spending and growth that, if continued unchecked, will—not *might* but *will*—change our country from a place where every generation does better than the last into a place where every generation piles more debt and more burden on the next.

Now, when politicians start talking about a brewing "crisis" in the land, most Americans rightly reach for their wallets. We're getting far too used to the overheated rhetoric of crisis and redemption coming from Washington. But there's something different about the challenge we face today. It's not a phony "crisis" Washington is cooking up to sell the public on its latest big government scheme. The message is being sent from the people to Washington today, not the other way around. Americans are anxious about their own financial futures and the country's financial future. They're worried about a government that is getting bigger and more controlling, and yet somehow still not addressing the issues they most care about.

Last February, about a year into the Obama presidency, a remarkable poll came out that sent this message loud and clear. CNN conducted a national survey in which a majority of Americans said they believe the federal government has become so large and so powerful it is trampling on their rights as ordinary citizens. Let me say it again—*most Americans believe government is so big it is depriving them of their rights.* As you might expect, more Republicans feel this way than Democrats, but a remarkable 63 percent of independents said they also believe their government is a threat to them. By overwhelming margins, Americans told CNN that they believe their government is broken. But in typical American fashion, overwhelming margins also hold out hope that their government can be fixed.

Paul, Kevin, and I don't "hold out hope" that America can get back on track, we *know* it can. But we're not about happy talk and empty promises. Americans bet on hope and change in 2008, but it hasn't worked out as promised. That doesn't mean, however, that the voters will automatically turn around and put their money on the other party. The need for a change in direction is urgent, but Americans are tired of gambling on soaring rhetoric and unfulfilled promises. They're feeling played by Washington and the special interests that control so many of the state capitals. The next group of leaders to get their vote is going to have to earn it the old-fashioned way: with real solutions to real problems.

———— ★ ————

I remember the moment I realized my party had lost its way. It was the morning of November 6, 2005. I opened the Sunday paper and saw the cover of *Parade* magazine. It featured a full color mock-up of the infamous "Bridge to Nowhere" in Alaska, the bridge that was to become the national symbol of an out-of-control Congress drunk on pork barrel spending.

Under the headline "Are Your Tax Dollars Being Wasted?" the *Parade* article described how, the previous summer, Congress had appropriated $223 million to build a bridge from Ketchikan, Alaska (population 8,200), to tiny Gravina Island (population 50). This lavish gift from

Washington, the magazine reported, amounted to $23,000 for each and every resident of Ketchikan.

The nation was still reeling from the scenes of devastation and corresponding government incompetence we all saw in the aftermath of Hurricane Katrina. Washington had not exactly covered itself in glory in response to that disaster, and now Americans were learning that Congress was writing $223 million checks to obscure towns in Alaska with well-connected congressional representatives. I thought to myself, "What does anyone in Richmond—or Miami, Dayton, Denver, or anywhere else, for that matter—care about a bridge in Alaska and why should they be asked to pay for it?"

In retrospect, the signs that the Republican Party had become the party of Washington—instead of the party that wanted to change Washington—had been around for some time. I'm not one who blindly follows polls, but as part of the leadership in the Republican-controlled Congress, even before the *Parade* cover I had been noticing that we were receiving steadily declining performance reports from the American people. There was a distance developing between my party and the people we were sworn to serve. Those who were a proud part of the Reagan Revolution no longer recognized the party he left behind. Week after week and month after month, the news got worse. Even for someone more inclined to follow his principles than the polls, it was an ominous development.

Somehow, in those months and years, my Republican

colleagues and I began to realize that the principles that we thought we were about just weren't being borne out in what was coming out of Washington. Life in the capital can be insulating. It can be hard to know how much of what goes on inside the beltway, under the Capitol Dome, really penetrates out there in America. After all, people have lives to live, jobs to get to, families to raise. America, sensibly in my view, looks to Washington to do the basics—provide for the common defense, keep the playing field level, spend as little as possible of their money—spend it wisely—and stay out of their way. But when I saw the *Parade* cover I realized that not only were we not living up to that expectation, we were going in the opposite direction. And Americans knew it. The public was clearly paying attention to what was going on in Washington—and they didn't like what they were seeing. Americans were coming to the conclusion that we no longer shared their desire for a less intrusive government, were no longer serious about fiscal responsibility, and no longer stood tall as the party of reform. And once the American people lost their trust in us, it wasn't too long before they didn't renew our lease in the Capitol.

What had gone wrong? Republicans had earned control of Congress in the Gingrich Revolution of 1994 by offering a clear, accountable alternative to business as usual. It's already hard to remember, but 1994 was the first time since 1952 that Republicans had a majority in the House of Representatives. For forty years, there had been one party rule in the House. How did congressional Democrats in Washington hold onto power for so long? By building a machine dedicated to delivering pork-barrel funds to the liberal special interests that delivered the votes to keep them in power, that's how. This is the corruption that is at the heart of every political machine. Any notion of a common good—or a principle more important than the perpetuation of the machine itself—is lost. Power becomes the object of governing, not listening to and responding to the concerns of the people.

It was only a matter of time before this corruption caught up with the Democratic majority, and by the early 1990s catch up with them it did. In 1989, Democrat Jim Wright became the first House Speaker to resign because of scandal. He was followed by Democratic whip Tony Coelho soon after. Then came the House banking scandal and the post office scandal, which led to the jailing of Ways and Means Committee chairman Dan Rostenkowski. Democrats had been in power so long they no longer felt the rules applied to them.

In 1994, the Contract with America promised an end to all that; it promised an end to the lack of accountability and an end to arrogant Washington congressional lifers taking and spending the people's money with impunity. The Contract with America made ten promises to the American people. Elect us, it said, and hold us accountable for making sure that the laws that apply to the country apply equally to Congress; make sure we open up committee meetings to the public and balance the budget. If we don't fulfill our promises, kick us out. If we do and you let us stay, we'll stick around as long as we have something useful to contribute to the country.

But the revolution of 1994 wasn't just about the slate of policy reforms to make Washington live under the rules that the rest of American has to live with. The Contract with America and the spirit of change it represented also drew a different kind of Republican public servant to Congress. These men and women weren't the same kind of Washington lifers and timeservers that had dominated the sclerotic Democratic majority. They were what Paul and Kevin and I call "citizen legislators." They were ordinary people, not political professionals. Doctors. Small businessmen. Veterans—men and women from all different walks of life. The 1994 election brought in Republicans like Tom Coburn of Oklahoma, a practicing obstetrician who pledged to serve only three terms in the House, did so, left office, and is now a United States Senator. Also in the House, North Carolina businesswoman Sue Myrick was elected, as well as Texas rancher Mac Thornberry and Arizona attorney John Shadegg.

The Republican class of 1994 in the House of Representatives delivered on every one of its promises in the Contract with America. They kept their word. Not every item in the Contract was enacted into law, but every single one received a fair hearing, an open debate, and an up or down vote. Not only that, but they worked with a Democratic president, Bill Clinton, to reform welfare on Republican terms. They provided proof that good ideas and goodwill can bridge the partisan divide in Washington. That's the way the system is supposed to work, whichever party is in charge. That's the way the American people expect it to work, and deserve for it to work. And for those promising weeks and months around the 1994 elections, the system did work.

But once much of the Contract had been fulfilled, and the votes had been taken and the promises kept, business in Washington slowly began to revert to business as usual. As the years went by, congressional Republicans began to give in to the temptations that had been the undoing of their predecessors. The leadership of the party changed, and slowly but surely, the GOP began to build their own political machine to match the Democratic machine they had replaced. Republicans were becoming more concerned with winning than governing. But the two go hand in hand.

The 1994 election had been a message from America to Washington. Americans are principled, but we're not ideologues. We don't put politics first and foremost in our lives, but we are a center-right nation. I believe the principles of my party best represent the principles of a center-right nation. We are the party of limited government, of free markets, and family values. But when Republicans finally achieved a measure of control in Washington, too often they left these principles behind. They became what they had campaigned against: arrogant and out of touch. There were important exceptions, but the GOP legislative agenda became primarily about Republican members themselves, not the greater cause.

That's what the current earmark culture is all about. It's the fuel that feeds the political machine. In the machine, you get your piece of the pie to keep yourself in power and you do the same for your fellow members. The implicit deal among members of the machine is this: you scratch my back and I'll scratch yours; you support my pork projects and I'll be there to support yours. Both parties have been guilty of this. And for both parties, the result has been the same: the illegal corruption of the process leads to members indicted and behind bars, and the legal corruption of the process leads to voters tossing out the incumbent party.

I witnessed this culture first hand when I came to Congress in 2001. Washington DC is just 110 miles up the road from my hometown of Richmond, but it may as well have been 10,000 miles away.

There I was, proud and privileged to be the representative from the 7th District of Virginia. I had been elected to the congressional seat once held by James Madison. But what I encountered in Washington DC was anything but Madisonian.

I had come *from* a place that, while not perfect, values and encourages entrepreneurialism. I had come *to* a place that knows little and seems to care even less about the struggles of small businesspeople.

I had come *from* a place that believes in hard work being

rewarded. I had come *to* a place where special interests are rewarded.

In Virginia, we reject intolerance and respect religious liberty. We don't spend money we don't have. And we understand the need for accountability, be it in ourselves, our children, or our local communities.

But these days Washington is engaged in an assault on religion in the public square. They're spending like there's no tomorrow. And accountability is something they seem to insist on only for the previous administration, not for themselves.

Needless to say, the culture shock for me in first encountering the nation's capital was pretty severe. I felt a little like George Taylor, Charlton Heston's character in the *Planet of the Apes* must have upon discovering the foundering Statue of Liberty on the beach. What was happening to my country?

———— ★ ————

I am the grandson of immigrants, and, as such, my life has been blessed with both the strong religious faith and hard working, entrepreneurial ethic that so many immigrants bring to America.

My paternal grandmother's family came to America the way so many of our forefathers and foremothers did—

penniless and proud. Her family fled Russia amid the anti-Semitism and bloody pogroms that preceded the Bolshevik Revolution.

My grandmother, who was widowed at a young age, lived at the corner of St. James and Charity streets in downtown Richmond, in a historically African-American neighborhood, where she raised two children above a tiny grocery store that she owned and operated. She worked day and night and sacrificed tremendously to secure a better future for her children. And sure enough, this young woman whose family had the courage to journey to a distant land with hope as their only possession—lifted herself into the ranks of the middle class. Through hard work, thrift, and faith, she was even able to send her two children to college.

It was through my grandmother's eyes that I developed a vision of America and its promise. In its purest sense, America is about looking forward. It's about the quest for freedom and opportunity. It's about persevering to pass on something better for your children than you inherited.

And if my belief in the American principles of freedom, opportunity, and tolerance come from my grandmother, the home that I have found for my principles in the Republican Party is thanks to one of the children she raised in that Richmond storefront: my father, Eddie Cantor.

People often ask me how I came to be a minority within a minority—an American who is not only Jewish but also a Republican. The short answer is—contrary to the myth of the Republican Party as bigoted and intolerant—my experience has been that it is the party for all Americans who want an opportunity to build a better future for their children and grandchildren.

I know, because it was the Republican Party that gave my father the opportunity to provide a better life for me and my family. Virginia in the 1950s and 1960s was not as open and tolerant a place as it is now. My mom and dad saw firsthand the racial segregation that was the norm at the time. They used to tell me the story of how, after they were married and my mother moved to Virginia from Baltimore, she boarded a bus in Richmond one day and took a seat in the back. Unfortunately, my dad was forced to direct her to the front of the bus because whites didn't sit in the back of the bus in those days.

And this fact didn't sit well with my father. At the time, Virginia was controlled—and had been controlled since the 1920s—by a Democratic political machine headed by the powerful Byrd family. Known simply as "the Organization," the Byrd organization did much to instill a limited government, low-taxation culture in Virginia. But in the 1950s and early 1960s, the Organization was a force of resistance to the growing civil rights movement, including resisting integrating Virginia's public schools.

My father rejected the politics of racial discrimination. And it was in the small but growing Virginia Republican Party that my father found a home. The Republican Party was a place where he could be accepted and supported, both as an American Jew and as an entrepreneur. It was the party that shared his belief in the conservative principles of family values and economic freedom.

Growing up, I came to share these values as well, but not for any lack of debate in the Cantor household. My mother and her Baltimore family were what the media would call considerably more "progressive" in their views than my father and his family. I remember trips to Virginia Beach and Ocean City with them that featured raucous debates about the issues of the day. It was my first exposure to politics.

My parents and grandparents also gave me a healthy exposure to the opportunities and the optimism that come with economic freedom, the type of opportunities that make our country so special, so unique, and so very different from any other in the history of human kind. Like my grandmother before me, I was then, and consider myself to this day, first and foremost a small businessperson. My first business was in real estate development and I learned the lesson that far too many small businessmen and -women learn when they try to be job creators: the process is tough, and the bureaucracy makes it tougher. In the process of building my business, I had encounters with regulators and bureaucrats who seemed completely disconnected to what it takes to run a business. They seemed to not know—or not care—what it takes to put your name on the line with a bank, what it takes to make a payroll, to pay taxes, and provide health-care benefits—all while constantly being held to account by whether you can afford to stay in business.

For anyone with a background in business, Washington DC can be a frustrating, even infuriating place. Talk about being disconnected from the realities of creating and maintaining jobs (if you're not using the taxpayer money to do it, that is). In 2009, a J.P. Morgan research report examined the private sector business experience of Washington presidential cabinet officials since 1900 and found the current administration to have the least private sector experience of all the presidential administrations studied. The report looked at the secretaries of State, Commerce, Treasury, Agriculture, Interior, Labor, Transportation, Energy, and Housing and Urban Development. It excluded postmaster general, and the secretaries of Navy, War, Homeland Security, Veterans Affairs, and Health, Education, and Welfare, because they don't have much to do with determining economic policy. Its findings were astonishing: over 90 percent of the prior experience of Obama administration cabinet officials was in the public sector. In other words, they were well schooled in the ways of government and the bureaucracy but few ever had to meet a payroll.

Now, there are some virtues to having a strong background in government. But in the midst of 10 percent-plus unemployment and the worst economic crisis since the Great Depression, resumes peppered with stints at HHS, USDA, DOJ, and the CCTP are not what we need. At a time when Americans desperately need jobs and job creators, we have a government of bureaucrats and regulators. No doubt there are good and conscientious bureaucrats and regulators. But think about what this means for a minute. A good day for a bureaucrat—a day of doing his job well—is a day that is most likely spent enforcing regulations, collecting taxes, and creating hurdles for entrepreneurs to jump through. It's not a day spent lowering taxes, breaking down barriers, and creating economic space for small business.

This administration just doesn't understand small businesspeople. And Congress isn't any better. The Democrats who control Congress, like House Speaker Nancy Pelosi (D-CA) are the most liberal of the liberal—way to the left of the American people and more liberal, even, than the Democratic rank and file. Many of the committee chairs, like Rep. Henry Waxman of California, the chairman of the powerful House Energy and Commerce Committee, have been in Congress for over thirty years. Rep. Charlie Rangel of New York, who has been forced to step down as the chairman of the all powerful Ways and Means Committee, has been in Washington since 1971, when Paul Ryan was a year old. In other words, the people who are making the nation's energy and tax policy for America's small business haven't been in the private sector for over three decades. Even if they were inclined to take the private sector's perspective, they wouldn't be able to remember what it is.

———— ★ ————

Growing up an American Jew in the South also taught me that America is about diversity. Not the corrupted notion of diversity that is fashionable today, which says we are all in racial or ethnic straightjackets from which we can't escape. I mean the American notion of diversity best expressed by those words "E Pluribus Unum"—"Out of many, one"—on the quarter in your pocket. To me, that says to the world that America is about opportunity and individual freedom. I've always believed that being an American is 85 percent about what you want to seek in life. The other 15 percent is the knowledge that there are Americans who are different from you and you have to have a tolerance for those differences. Far from being a handicap, being a Republican Jew has shown me what is best in America. You can be a minority within a minority and still make your way in this country.

In America there are no limits—that's the message that Paul and Kevin and I are working so hard to communicate. That's the kind of country we are working to preserve. There's a powerful force in our politics today that rejects this view of America. It believes that individual Americans are, for the most part, victims in need of a nanny state. What's worse, these voices in our politics are all too prone to demonize those who disagree with them. They label dissent, not as patriotism, but as jingoism or, far worse, racism.

No one is claiming the United States of America is perfect, and we most certainly have our faults like any other nation. But we are at the same time not like any other nation. We have a unique set of founding, guiding principles that have made us great, despite our faults. No party has a monopoly on virtue. Public servants and private citizens who genuinely love this country and want the best for it exist in both parties. But I believe that it is the Republican Party whose principles best capture what has made America great. It is with the conservative principles of individual liberty, economic freedom, and support for families that America's future rests. If I didn't believe this was true, I wouldn't call myself a Republican.

And that is why it is such a tragedy that Republicans in Washington fell short of our principles in the past.

The fact is, we had our chance, and we blew it. For Paul, Kevin, and me, America is about getting a fair chance to succeed or fail; it's about giving individuals the freedom to soar to new heights as well as giving them the security they need when they fall down. This is what Americans want from their government. And what were we offering? A Bridge to Nowhere.

We got what we had coming.

CHAPTER TWO

A Year of Living Dangerously

———— ★ ————

I may never again have as good a seat as I had on Inauguration Day, January 20, 2009. I was seated on the front steps of the Capitol, in the second row, with a bird's-eye view of the president and his family as President Obama was sworn in. From my vantage point I could also look out at the sea of Americans stretching all the way back to the Washington Monument. Best of all, I could see the faces of the President and First Lady's two young daughters, Sasha and Malia, as their father participated in the peaceful transfer of government that made him the most powerful man in the world. I found myself in awe, not only of the sight of the over one million Americans who had come to Washington that cold January day, but of my own privilege to be present for history in the making.

Barack Obama hadn't been my candidate, but now he

was my president. Like many conservatives, I was fully aware of the message the American people had sent at the polls in November. Truthfully, it had been one of the most bitter and disappointing elections that I can remember. Combined with the thrashing we took at the polls in 2006, Republicans in the House of Representatives had lost 54 seats by the end of 2008—that's 54 fewer votes we had to shape the future of the country, the future for my children—Jenna, Michael, and Evan—and the future for your children.

To be honest, I couldn't blame the voters for cutting us off at the knees. The American economy was in free fall. Millions of Americans were losing their jobs. Businesses were struggling to keep the lights on, much less meet their payrolls. So far, Washington had responded with what the American people perceived as a big business bailout that put Wall Street before Main Street. Americans were worried about their economic security, and increasingly, they were convinced that the playing field wasn't level. They had seen crooks like Bernie Madoff cheating investors. They had seen corporations like AIG take taxpayer funds and award their executives fat bonuses. They had seen their government in bed with big business, privatizing gains and socializing losses. And through it all, the only people who seemed to pay the bill for all of this were the hard-working Americans who didn't have lobbying shops in Washington DC.

Before the 110th Congress had adjourned the year before, Republicans in the House had elected me to the number two position in the Republican leadership: Republican whip. And from the time of Barack Obama's victory at the polls, my colleagues and I in the leadership had stood ready to work with the new administration. The immediate situation facing our nation required serious leadership, and while we held out hope that the president-elect's "post-partisan" rhetoric was indeed serious, we weren't kidding ourselves. We knew we had serious areas of disagreement with the president-elect. We also knew that he faced a choice: would he, as promised, change the ways of Washington and make the tough decisions necessary to return America to long-term growth and fiscal sustainability? Or would he lead under the old liberal guise that massive spending binges equal meaningful reform?

There were signs—words, at any rate—that gave us some measure of hope in those early days. I remember vividly President-elect Obama declaring in December 2008, "What we don't know yet is whether my administration and this next generation of leadership is going to be able to hew a new, more pragmatic approach that is less interested in whether we have big government or small government than in *whether we have a smart, effective government.*"

Smart and effective government is something I'm all for. I just happen to believe that the adjectives "smart" and "effective" when applied to the noun "government" require a third adjective: "small." You don't have to look any further than history—both American history and the history of countries with more expansive government—to see that government that works is *limited* government.

For decades, Western European countries have followed a high tax, big entitlement, big government model that has left them with high levels of permanent unemployment and stagnant economies. In Europe, for every euro spent by businesses to employ a worker, an average of only 40 cents makes its way into the employee's paycheck. The remaining 60 cents goes to the taxes that pay for the cradle-to-grave European nanny state. The economic crisis in Greece is the future of Europe. I could never understand why so many of my Democratic colleagues in the House seemed to think this was the path that our America should follow.

In these countries, democracy has been subverted by what columnist George Will calls the "dependency agenda." The dependency agenda aims to make citizens so dependent on government that they support its expansion and resist its contraction. By making more and more people look to government for their health care, their retirement, and even their jobs, the party of the dependency agenda guarantees its continued success as long as it supports more and bigger government. In the countries that have adopted the dependency agenda, self-government has become virtu-ally meaningless. The expansion of government becomes self-fulfilling. Anyone or any party who advocates cutting back on government and government spending is commit-ting political suicide.

Historically, (thankfully!) America has resisted this

European model. For all its recent problems, the American economy doesn't suffer the systemic problems that the European economies have. We don't have chronic high levels of unemployment and, at least historically, our government spending hasn't been so high that it crowds out spending and investment in the private sector. America is the land of promise, prosperity, and opportunity. But big government did not make it so.

Winston Churchill once said that, "Some see private enterprise as a predatory target to be shot, others as a cow to be milked, but few are those who see it as a sturdy horse pulling the wagon." Count me among Churchill's "few."

Why have our small businesses, entrepreneurs, and workers been so motivated to work hard and innovate over the years? Because hard work in America was rewarded. Why have investors and job creators around the world gravitated to U.S. capital markets? Because America was a place where taxes and regulations fostered competitiveness, transparency, and accountability. Why have countries around the world made the U.S. dollar the world's reserve currency? Because America was a rock of financial stability that pursued sound fiscal policies.

So as I sat in the cold January sun and listened to the new president's inaugural speech, I wasn't really sure what kind of president Barack Obama would be. And throughout the day as I talked to people who had come to the capital to be present at the inauguration, I knew I wasn't alone. Everyone was proud that our country was inaugurating its first African American president. But beyond that, many Americans I talked to in Washington that day didn't seem to know much more about the man they had just made their leader. There was a celebratory atmosphere in the capital. But who exactly were we celebrating?

———— ★ ————

The answer came surprisingly quickly, in the battle over the American Recovery and Reinvestment Act, better known as the stimulus bill.

Our Republican congressional team had emerged from the November elections with virtually no power to control the legislative agenda. In the House, on January 3, 2009, our über minority began:

* 178 House Republicans (just 40 percent of the House's total membership)
* A 9-to-4 disadvantage on the Rules Committee, the body responsible for bringing bills to the floor and deciding what issues are debated
* House Delegates or Resident Commissioners (of which there are 6, who, thanks to the Democratic majority, are now allowed to vote on amendments on the House floor)

In the Senate, Democrats had a strong majority, enough votes to guarantee passage of anything they wanted, provided they stuck together.

But despite our battered status, we knew our number one priority—regardless of which party we belonged to— was to do what we could do to help get Americans back to work and get the economy back on track. Unemployment was at a sixteen-year high of 7.2 percent. And the Congressional Budget Office was reporting that the annual deficit was on track to climb to its highest point since World War II, to $1.2 trillion or 8 percent of the nation's entire economic output—and that *wasn't* including taxpayers' funds spent on the stimulus.

Politics can be tough, and no party is above seeking its advantage where it can. But the degree to which Americans were suffering under the recession was, for us House Republicans, our primary concern in January 2009. Rather than be an obstacle to action to get Americans back to work, we were determined to use the full force of our ideas to help the Democratic majority produce a better stimulus bill to help pull the country back from the economic abyss. There would be nothing we could do that would be more damaging to the country—as well as our prospects as a party—than to conform to the Democrats' desperate attempts to portray us as the party of "no." We knew we had a better way to get the economy going again, and we weren't shy about sharing it.

A group of us—including Paul, Kevin, Rep. Peter Roskam of Illinois, Rep. Jeb Hensarling of Texas, Rep. Dave Camp of Michigan, Rep. Shelley Moore Capito of West Virginia, Rep. Chris Lee of New York, Rep. Judy Biggert of Illinois, Rep. John Campbell of California, Rep. Tom Price of Georgia, and me—had been meeting for weeks in my conference room in the Capitol to develop a plan for job growth. We had three ironclad criteria for our alternative stimulus bill as well as any other bills designed to "rescue" the economy: they had to be limited in scope and spending; they had to focus on creating real, sustainable jobs; and they had to put small businesses first.

For me, the principles that guided me in trying to help fix the economy were the ones I had learned as a small businessman. Government doesn't create jobs and build wealth; entrepreneurs, risk takers, and private businesses do. But throughout a series of meetings with Obama administration officials on the stimulus bill, it became clear that they didn't share this belief. The president's team were fervent believers in the economic theories of a British economist called John Maynard Keynes, whose theories were developed in the early-to-mid-twentieth century. Keynesian theory says that government can create jobs and spur economic development simply by spending—even spending money it doesn't have. The idea is that government can be counted on to spend more wisely than the people. By taking more of the taxpayers' money—or borrowing or simply printing more money—and then spending it as the government sees fit, jobs will be created and the economy will grow.

Or so the theory goes.

Paul, Kevin, and I rejected this approach. We believed then as we believe now: it is small businesses—driven to innovate, invest, and grow—that will regenerate the millions of sustainable jobs we so desperately need. Since every dollar government spends comes from the private sector via the taxpayers, our test of worthwhile public spending is this: will the return be greater if these funds are spent by the government or if they are left in the private sector to be spent and invested? In most cases, government spending fails this test, and the Democratic stimulus bill was no exception. We believed any bill designed to put Americans back to work needed to take bold steps to encourage work, investment, and business expansion, something that government spending under Keynesian economic theory too often fails to provide.

To put our belief to the test of a practical plan to achieve economic growth, our group, called the House Republican Economic Recovery Working Group,* held a series of exhaustive meetings. We reached out into the private sector and held hearings featuring former eBay Chief Executive Officer Meg Whitman and former Massachusetts governor and businessman Mitt Romney. We heard from dozens of small businessmen and -women. More than twenty members of Congress participated in our deliberations. And we took advantage of new technologies to reach as many par-

---

*For a full list of members, see Appendix A.

ticipants as possible. We used Facebook and YouTube to allow people to submit questions. And we put video of our proceedings online for what may just be the first YouTube series of congressional hearings.

Then, on January 23, 2009, in a meeting with the president and his economic advisers in the Roosevelt Room of the White House, Republican leader John Boehner and I presented the president with our alternative stimulus bill.

Now, it's important at this point to say a thing or two about protocol in Washington. When you're invited to a meeting at someone else's house—in this case, the White House—you generally don't bring handouts. You generally let your host determine the agenda. But we had worked very hard, and the stakes were very high. Besides, as President-elect Barack Obama had himself said, no one party has a monopoly on good ideas. That had encouraged us. We had good ideas. So I made sure I was polite when, at that White House meeting, I said, "Mr. President with your permission, I'd like to hand something out." And with that, I passed out copies of our five-point alternative stimulus plan.

What we proposed at that meeting could not have been more different than the bloated $787 billion monstrosity that was eventually passed by the Democratic Congress. It was a simple, direct way to create jobs and help our economy by focusing on small businesses. Here are the highlights of the plan I handed the president:

★ Reducing the lowest individual tax rates from 15 percent to 10 percent and from 10 percent to 5 percent

★ Allowing small business to reduce its tax liability by 20 percent

★ Ensuring no tax increases to pay for spending

★ Assistance for the unemployed

★ A home-buyers credit of $7,500 for those buyers who can make a minimum down payment of 5 percent

Not only was our plan fair, understandable, and more direct than the Democratic majority's bill, it delivered twice the bang for half the bucks spent in the Democratic plan. In fact, Ways and Means Ranking Member Dave Camp of Michigan and his staff used the Obama administration's own economic model to analyze our alternative stimulus bill that they determined would create twice the jobs at half the cost of the bill that was eventually passed.

After I handed him the plan, President Obama's response was encouraging, albeit in a backhanded kind of way. "Eric, there's nothing too crazy in here," he said. And he was right, of course.

We genuinely wanted to find a way to produce the best economic recovery bill we could. Paul, Kevin, and I and the other members of the House Republican Economic Recovery Working Group purposefully checked our ideology at the door when we formulated our plan. Would we have much preferred a bill that eliminated the business income tax and lowered all tax rates? You bet we would have. But we didn't come into the meeting naïve enough to think that the new administration would follow such a plan, rejecting their own Keynesian beliefs. We knew that they would dismiss a Republican plan like that out of hand. Instead, we were realistic and we made an honest, good faith effort to work with the administration and came with an incremental, pro-small-business, and free-market alternative.

Helping small businesses, the engine of job creation, was of special concern to us. One of the ways we proposed to alleviate the tax burden they face each and every day was by reducing the effective tax rate by 20 percent. The mom-and-pop stores and restaurants that I visited at home in my district were telling me this was the tax break they needed to invest in new equipment or new hires.

So there I was, explaining to President Obama and his economic brain trust—including Office of Management and Budget director Peter Orszag, chief economic adviser Larry Summers and Chief of Staff Rahm Emanuel—what deli owners, shopkeepers, and service providers in Richmond were telling me they needed. And as the meeting continued, I could tell the president's team wasn't getting it. Even though these were some of the smartest people in the country, they were *entirely* disconnected from the realities and concerns of small businessmen and -women.

They were all talented, conscientious public servants, but their experience—and their hearts—just weren't in the private sector. To put it another way, *this was an administration of the government, by the government, and for the government*—not entrepreneurs or the private sector.

Still, we had what the press in Washington calls a "frank exchange" of views and ideas in the meeting. The Republicans present argued that lifting the tax burden on individuals and businesses was needed to create jobs. But instead of doing that, while we tried to reason with the president, Appropriations Committee chairman David Obey (D-MI) and the Democratic leadership in Congress had turned the stimulus bill into a bloated grab bag of taxpayer-funded government gifts to special interests. How could we support a bill that spends $12 on new cars for the federal government for every $1 in tax relief to small businesses? How could we expect a bill that contains a whopping $219 billion that the Congressional Budget Office had told us wouldn't be spent until October 1, 2010—over a year and a half away—to stimulate the economy now?

For their part, President Obama and his advisers said that while they shared our desire to kick-start the economy, on some issues we were just going to have ideological differences. Fair enough, I thought. We *do* have differences, and I took them at their word that they were willing to work with us to iron them out for the good of the country. But then, the president played a trump card that, although I didn't know it at the time, foreshadowed the battle to come.

After sparring for a bit on tax policy he stopped and said simply, "Elections have consequences . . . and *Eric,* I *won.*"

In other words: it's my way or the highway. Deal with it. The "post-partisan" president sure had a big partisan streak.

──────── ★ ────────

Later, President Obama and his spokespeople would describe our opposition to the stimulus bill as our coming out as the party of "no." I well remember meeting later with the president in the Cabinet Room of the White House (ironically, at a supposedly "bipartisan" gathering of House and Senate leaders) in which he accused us Republicans of making a calculated, political decision to oppose him on the stimulus bill instead of doing what was right for the country. He charged then (incorrectly), as he later would repeatedly, that we had already made the decision to oppose the stimulus bill before we even heard his proposals. "Stop listening to Rush Limbaugh," he scolded us, "and do what's right for the people."

It was too much for me to listen to without speaking up. I reminded the president that, despite his assurances that he was ready to work with us on an economic stimulus bill, he had outsourced the actual creation of the bill to House Speaker Nancy Pelosi and Senate majority leader Harry Reid. They had produced—without allowing any input from us—a near trillion-dollar-high tidal wave of cash pouring into the Democrats' favored programs. It was *that* bill, one that was actually introduced the night *before* we were to meet with him in the Capitol to discuss the stimulus, that the press had reported that we would oppose. And it was that bill, drafted by the majority leadership—without any opportunity for Republican input—that was forced to a vote in the House the very next day.

Far from us having made a political decision to oppose the president, the liberal House leadership had made the political decision to draft the bill without our input and ideas, and the president had made the decision to allow them to do so—all the while insisting that he was ready to work with us on getting Americans back to work. When we met with the president in the Capitol, we were ready to work with him to forge a bipartisan bill. Instead, President Obama embraced the partisan Democratic leadership bill and went on to accuse us of bad faith.

In retrospect, it's easy to see why the White House political brain trust would pursue a strategy of having the president speak happy words of compromise while the Democratic leadership did the dirty work of shutting out Republican ideas from the bill. President Obama's approval ratings at the time were in the stratosphere. Somewhere around 70 percent of the American people approved of him personally at the end of January 2009. Washington insiders and media pundits thought it was insane to oppose so popular a president on a bill that spread so much money around. *Time* magazine wrote that, "flagrantly opposing a wildly popular new President is risky, especially when any payoff could take years." And unnamed White House officials even whispered to the media that we would pay the price for opposing business groups who supported the Democratic stimulus bill in the fatalistic belief that only government spending could jump-start the economy.

I will let history judge whether government spending is the best way to spur job creation and economic growth, much less whether the $787 billion Democratic stimulus bill did much to help our economy. But sometimes saying "No" is what's right for this country—and all 178 Republican members said just that to President Obama, Speaker Pelosi, and Leader Reid's pork-laden stimulus package. At the same time, we did so after offering our own, better alternative, which was central to creating a sense of purpose and unity among House Republicans—we were going to be the party of principled opposition.

Still, back in January 2009, we knew we were taking a gamble when we decided, as a group of House Republicans, to oppose the stimulus bill. We knew the Democrats had the votes in the House to pass the legislation without us. But if they were able to gain the support of just two or three Republican members, they would be able to put a phony "bipartisan" label on the bill and claim it was passed, not on behalf of favored Democratic special interest groups, but on behalf of the American people. And as for business groups who misguidedly supported the bill, our position was clear cut: our obligation was, first and foremost, to the people. Our job was to be prudent guardians of the taxpayers' money, not to line up like robots behind self-proclaimed business interests.

In the end, the stimulus bill passed the House of Representatives on January 28, 2009, without a single Republican vote. In the Senate, just three Republicans—Maine Senators Olympia Snowe and Susan Collins, and then-Republican Arlen Specter of Pennsylvania—supported the bill.

As the Republican Whip, my job was to try to convince my colleagues in the House that it was in the nation's interest—as well as their own interest—to oppose the bill. However, the Whip Team didn't take the old-style approach—breaking arms and cutting deals—to bring us all together. Instead, we came together by developing sound, principled, commonsense solutions and alternatives that resulted in a better way that was a credible alternative to the Democrats' plan. This model would become the hallmark of how we would engage the Democrat majority going forward—saying no to bad policies by offering a credible alternative.

The Democratic majority hadn't produced a stimulus bill; it had produced a spending bill. In contrast, we had worked hard to produce a serious, forward-looking, smarter, and simpler plan to create real, sustainable jobs. We gave our members what they needed to go home to their Rotary Clubs and their chambers of commerce and neighborhood meetings and say, "Here's the Democratic bill, it costs more than the entire Iraq War, will give us budget deficits not seen since World War II, and most of the spending won't even reach the economy for over a year. But here's our bill, and it's a better way." We gave our members what they needed to be viewed as leaders, as sensible, responsible legislators trying to address problems and fight back against this notion that if we didn't just accept the Democratic plan than we were the party of "no."

So in a sense, President Obama had been correct when he identified the stimulus vote as a turning point—he was just wrong about what message it sent to the American people. Far from revealing us as the party of "no," our solidarity in the face of the majority party's bullying tactics revealed us to be an awakening movement of responsible leaders; the adults in the room at a reckless liberal blowout on the taxpayers' dime. The mainstream media didn't like it one bit, of course. The snarky *New York Times* columnist Maureen Dowd complained that "somehow the most well-known person on the planet lost control of the economic message to someone named Eric Cantor."

Getting under the skin of certain *New York Times* columnists is a badge of honor as far as I'm concerned. But there was no cause for celebration for anyone after the stimulus vote. For one thing, the majority Democrats were determined to make us pay a price for our opposition to the bill. Chris Van Hollen, the head of the Democrat Campaign Committee, had warned us that opposition to the stimulus bill would be the centerpiece of the Democrats' 2010 attack ads. And sure enough, once the bill passed, the Left embarked upon a very organized, sophisticated campaign attacking Republican opposition to their agenda.

One House colleague told me about going home to her district, only to wake up in the morning to see an ad on television attacking her. Then she opened the paper and went online and read the streams of vitriol financed by the Left. Getting in her car, she turned on the radio, hearing ads portraying her as someone she didn't recognize. And when she returned home at night she got more of the same through the mail and robo calls.

But the real reason we weren't patting ourselves on the back was that Americans were still out of work. Despite the Obama administration's promise that unemployment wouldn't reach over 8 percent if the stimulus passed, unemployment surged to over 10 percent as the year went on. Americans were hurting and all we had accomplished was to go $787 billion deeper in debt. Just three and a half months after it became law, the vice president bizarrely took to the microphone and announced that when it came to taxpayer's stimulus dollars, "There are going to be mistakes made, some people are being scammed already." And sadly that pattern hasn't changed. This wasn't the type of change most Americans expected—nor deserved.

House Republicans had always known that our belief in free people and free markets was the route to economic recovery. After the stimulus vote we had new confidence in

our ability—and our credibility with the American people—
to translate our beliefs into solutions. We just needed the
votes to get it done.

———————— ★ ————————

The massive stimulus bill was just the opening round in
a high spending, big government agenda, that over the
course of the last year and a half that has put at risk what
I consider to be the essence of the American Dream: leaving my children and grandchildren a better country and
the opportunity for a better life than what I inherited. As
Paul will detail later, America is approaching a point of no
return in which, if we don't change our ways, each year
we will pile more debt on future generations than the year
before. The policies of the past year and a half didn't create
this cascading cycle of spending and debt, but they have
dangerously accelerated it.

After the stimulus vote, nothing concrete had changed
in Washington. The liberal lifers were still in control of
Congress. President Obama was still popular. But something important had changed for my conservative colleagues
and me: our ability to stand together on the stimulus vote
had strengthened our resolve. We went on to stand unanimously against the president's big spending budget. We
sent a strong message that there is a better way to become

energy independent by maintaining strong opposition to the cap-and-trade bill. We had a new confidence. We were moving from playing defense to playing offense. We knew that the model we had followed with the stimulus bill—working hard to present our own commonsense solutions to contrast with the majority's big government proposals—was the best way forward.

A good example is the housing crisis. Soon after the stimulus bill, the Obama administration rolled out a housing plan that sought to alleviate the mortgage crisis by throwing enormous sums of good taxpayer money at people who had engaged in irresponsible and even fraudulent behavior to get a mortgage, but now weren't paying their bills.

From the outset of the housing crisis, Washington Democrats had done all they could to direct the public's anger away from one of the prime culprits in the crisis: the liberal special interest slush funds otherwise known as Fannie Mae and Freddie Mac. Democratic lawmakers, led by Financial Services chairman Barney Frank (D-MA), gambled with the taxpayers' money on millions of risky loans and then blamed everyone else when their house of cards fell down. Left out in the cold were the nine out of ten Americans who had behaved responsibly and were continuing to work hard, play by the rules, and pay their mortgages on time.

Again, far from being the party of no, we had a better way to keep honest, hard-working Americans in their homes and to stop the free fall in housing prices. To keep responsible homeowners who are at risk of losing their home through no fault of their own, such as those who find themselves temporarily out of work, we offered a $5,000 refinancing tax credit.

And instead of offering incentives for more irresponsible behavior, we offered incentives for Americans to buy new homes or refinance at a lower rate. Our plan included a $15,000 tax credit for the purchase of a primary home *provided that the buyer paid 5 percent down*. It also included incentives for lenders to keep owners in their homes by refinancing mortgages and lowering monthly payments. If the homeowner agreed to share a portion of future home appreciation with the lender, the lender would be exempted from taxes on eventual profits and the borrower would not pay taxes as the result of refinancing.

Our plan was very different from the administration's plan to have the taxpayers foot the bill for modifying mortgages. We believed that enough irresponsible financial behavior was being bailed out by Washington. It was time to stick up for the Americans who weren't walking away; those who were sacrificing to do the right thing and pay their mortgages.

We also differed—radically—from the Democrats in charge of Washington when it came to energy and the environment. Their cap-and-trade bill has rightly been called a cap-and-tax bill. It would essentially amount to a national energy tax that would slam small businesses with higher energy bills and put more pressure on already struggling middle-class American families. Even President Obama, during his presidential campaign, told the editorial board at the *San Francisco Chronicle* that the policy would cause electricity rates to "skyrocket." At a time of economic uncertainty and high unemployment, it's the last thing we need. And yet Speaker Pelosi and congressional Democrats have called it their number one priority.

All you have to do is look around you—and read a little history—to know that the best thing a nation can do for its environment is to generate wealth and prosperity. There aren't a lot of struggling, developing nations devoting their effort and resources to protecting the environment. And, contrary to all the fans of authoritarian regimes like China in the columns of the mainstream media, it's not the economies smothered by big government that are producing the innovations that will supply "green" energy.

There's a better way to protect our jobs and protect our environment—it's offering incentives to develop new energy technologies, not penalties for heating your home and operating your business. We need to protect our national security by developing *American* sources of energy like our clean natural gas and our abundant coal from shale. And we need to offer incentives for our companies to develop the alternative energy we need to make us energy independent. The last thing America's economy, our national security, or our environment needs is more taxes to kill jobs and stifle innovation. It is important that we diversify energy sources for both our economic and environmental security. And Republicans developed the American Energy Act, which shows that being conservative and green go hand in hand.

———— ★ ————

What is most heartbreaking for me looking back on the past year and a half is the wasted potential it represents. President Obama and the strengthened Democratic majority in Congress rode in on a wave of genuine hope for change in 2008. They could have reached across the aisle and found real solutions to our challenges. They could have helped find commonsense answers—answers that wouldn't satisfy the radical fringes of either party but would address the needs of the American people. Instead, they mistook the voters' disgust with Washington for a mandate for a Far-Left agenda. They decided, in the words of the White House chief of staff, to "never let a serious crisis go to waste" and attempted to exploit the country's economic anxiety to entrench huge new government entitlements.

President Obama has implored us to get beyond ideology and he's right. Americans don't care about dogma, be it of the Left or of the Right. They're not looking to belong to a club and know all the secret handshakes. They just want to live their lives and make better lives for their families.

But Americans have been watching Washington as the

Democrats have exercised one-party rule over their government, and they've noticed a pattern. Remember how, at the beginning of his presidency, President Obama insisted he didn't care if government was bigger or smaller, he just wanted it to be "smarter and more effective"? Well, it hasn't escaped any of us that every proposal from the Obama administration for ostensibly "better and smarter" government has called for *bigger* government. There have been no instances in which the administration has equated more effective government with smaller government. As far as the Democrats are concerned, the causality only runs one way—to a European-style welfare state.

This pattern started with the disaster of the stimulus bill—and then it got markedly worse, if you can believe that. As small businesses and families across the country tightened their belts, President Obama pushed an additional $3.6 trillion spending plan through Congress in its 2009 budget.

Then the Democrats got in the auto business. Instead of allowing its union cronies and corporate CEOs to be held accountable for their poor decisions, they made the taxpayers accountable by buying Chrysler and General Motors. It was the bailout culture all over again, with Washington privatizing gains and socializing losses.

As work began on health care in the spring of 2009, their "big government is better government" approach to America's problems came into sharp relief. Democrats and Republicans agree that our health-care system is broken in fundamental ways. We agree that costs are too high, putting health care out of reach to millions of Americans without insurance, and endangering the coverage of millions of Americans with health care.

We disagree fundamentally, however, on how to fix our system. As Paul and Kevin will go into detail later, we believe the patient and her doctor should be the decision makers when it comes to health care, not a bureaucrat in the basement of the Health and Human Services building in Washington DC.

Many of those in power in Washington feel differently and, no surprise, their answer has been for more and more expensive government. Far from "bending the cost curve down," their plan had a trillion-dollar price tag.

The result was, by June of 2009, President Obama and congressional Democrats had enacted or proposed policies that would accumulate more debt than was amassed by all the previous presidents in America's 220-year history. They had put us on an unsustainable financial path, with the debt set to double over the next five years and triple in ten years. Under their out-of-control spending, within three years the federal government will spend *$1 billion a day just on interest on the debt*. Within ten years we will spend $2 billion a day, just to tread financial water and keep ourselves afloat.

Americans are genuinely—and rightly—concerned about the debt we are piling on future generations. They're concerned about the country's financial future and their own financial future. But I believe this anxiety also captures a larger anxiety about the future of our country. When we debate issues like government spending and health care—or, worse, when we don't debate them and the majority party just forces its will on the country—we are really debating what kind of country we want to have. Will it be a place where the freedoms that have made us great are preserved and adopted to meet the challenges of the twenty-first century? Or will it be a place we don't recognize; a country whose citizens are so dependent on and enslaved by big government that we no longer control our own destinies? Will it be a country that keeps the playing field level and gives everyone the opportunity to work and succeed? Or will it be a place where our leaders rig the game in favor of the special interests who keep them in power?

These, I believe, were the fundamental questions on the minds of the voters as they went to the polls in the off-year elections in 2009 and the special Massachusetts election in early 2010. They were responding to the question, "What kind of country do we want to have?" And their answer was, simply, "Not the kind of country Washington has us headed toward today."

Pro-market, limited government candidates won in New Jersey, Virginia, and Massachusetts, not by running away from their principles and trying to pull a fast one on the voters, but by standing firm with their principles and offering solutions based on them. Independent voters flocked to Gov. Chris Christie, Gov. Bob McDonnell, and Sen. Scott Brown because they talked about jobs and opportunity for citizens and restraint and accountability for government.

Watching the celebration of Inauguration Day 2009, there were few who would have predicted the outcomes of the elections in Virginia, New Jersey, and Massachusetts less than a year later. President Obama and the congressional Democrats sold themselves to the American people as their best bet for hope and change. And they have not delivered.

A year and a half later, two things are increasingly clear: first, the need for a fundamental change in America's direction is more urgent than ever.

And second, there is a better way.

CHAPTER THREE

A Better Way

———— ★ ————

Paul, Kevin, and I are unapologetic believers in the concept of American exceptionalism. America offers opportunity like no other nation, and with hard work, sacrifice, and perseverance, no one is limited. After all, where else could people from such humble beginnings as Abraham Lincoln, Harry Truman, and Ronald Reagan even dream of growing up to become president? Our country is built on the notion that hard work, creativity, and responsible risk taking are rewarded. This is what we are fighting so hard to preserve.

Yet today, America rests in the hands of a Democratic majority that views America differently. They love their country, but it seems to me that they tend to focus on its flaws rather than its greatness. They crave the approval of the very international elites whose nations have never offered the opportunity that America has. And above all, they think America is an ordinary nation, not an exceptional nation in the way that tens of millions who risked their lives to come to our shores legally in search of the American dream saw it. They think America is just one nation among many, with few unique virtues, responsibilities, enemies, or destiny.

Time and again, they try to sell us on promises that just don't add up. They tell us that we can give all Americans health-care coverage and still save money—without fixing the fundamental antimarket character of our health-care system. They tell us that government can reward irresponsible borrowing and financial behavior and not encourage more of it. They say that we can spend all we want today and somehow not burden future generations of Americans with higher taxes and lower prospects. And they employ the politics of fear against anyone who suggests reforming our broken entitlements, scaring seniors and the needy into being their unwitting partners in the destruction of the very programs they say they want to save.

For the good of this nation and its future, we must change course. No longer can we run up the national credit card—either by necessity or design—which results in government taking more of what we earn, impeding small businesses, and consigning our children and grandchildren to less opportunity than we've had. We're headed for a country in which a paternalistic government that believes it knows better than we do dictates our most intimate choices, whether it's in our children's classrooms, our doctors' offices, or our family living rooms. It's a dangerous path on which liberty is forgotten and opportunity is lost.

I have complete faith in the good judgment of the American people to choose a different course. They're not only ready for adult leadership; they're ready to be talked to like adults. All Americans understand that we face difficult and serious challenges. But in the effort to rise above these challenges, they don't want their leaders to destroy our prized values and liberties; they want us to become more forceful advocates for them.

The good news is that there's a new generation of limited government, free-market leaders ready to move the country forward in a more prosperous direction.

Over the past year and a half, we have fought to restore the American people's trust by offering a policy-based alternative approach. In the face of a rigidly ideological Democratic agenda, we put forward principled opposition to drive the national debate back to the center—toward the commonsense solutions that this majority has eschewed.

These efforts have given the public a window on how we as a party will lead. Under a Republican Congress, Americans will see less Washington and more hope, opportunity, and freedom. We will present a positive agenda that harnesses this country's greatness and looks to its bright future.

Simply put: there is a better way.

★

We are a new generation of Republican leaders eager to put our past sins behind us. We pledge to stand on principle, to lead as adults and—most of all—to serve as responsible stewards of the public trust by listening to the American people.

That means getting back to our core principles and applying a basic test to all our actions on behalf of the American people. When we consider a domestic policy, we will first ask: does it create jobs, strengthen our long-term economic footing, and take a responsible approach to spending while shifting focus away from Washington to the people? Washington should be working for the people, not the other way around. And on the foreign policy front: does it protect the safety, security, and sovereignty of America and its allies while assessing current and future threats and developing clear strategies for addressing them?

Paul, Kevin, and I believe these types of litmus tests would signal a welcome change from the misplaced priorities of the current president, Speaker Pelosi, and Leader Reid.

Take it from me, the past eighteen months have been busy ones in Washington. The president and the Democratic leadership have frantically produced and lobbied for plans to tax energy, create government health care, close Guantánamo Bay, bail out corporations, and, of course, spend lots and lots of your money. The one thing they haven't done much about is the most important issue for Americans: jobs.

A headline about an upcoming presidential trip in the April 7 *Los Angeles Times* said it all: "Obama off to Prague to not talk U.S. jobs once more."

Republicans began offering a better way to get America back to work when the administration pushed through its budget-busting $787 billion (that became $862 billion) so-called stimulus plan. As I've written, our alternative bill would have created twice the jobs at half the cost of the Democratic bill, which, it must be repeated, has failed even on its own terms.

As we've said, there is a better way to create jobs for Americans and secure our children's future prosperity than taking more and more tax dollars out of the private sector and giving them to government to spend. Our jobs plan begins by rejecting this logic and reversing this trend. Small businessmen and -women tell me virtually every day that the threat of increased taxes, regulation, and government mandates are deterrents to business expansion and job growth. And they know of what they speak. During its first fifteen months, the Obama administration has considered more than one hundred separate regulations that would cost the economy—including small businesses—more than one million dollars each. Do you know any small businesses that can handle this type of crippling loss? Of course not.

For our economy to grow and create jobs, Washington needs to repeal any government regulation that will impose an economic cost, trigger job losses, or disproportionately impact small businesses. Our rule should be, first, do no harm! The same goes for job-killing federal tax increases. It's just common sense. You don't raise taxes during a period of high unemployment. Period. And while we're on the subject of taxes, the United States has the second highest tax in the world on the earnings of U.S. companies operating abroad. (This is actually describing two problems: we both have the second highest tax rate and we tax companies on their worldwide income as opposed to territorial income like most other countries.) Lowering that tax, even for a limited period of time, would encourage companies to bring their profits home and create new jobs instead of reinvesting them overseas.

Paul has been warning for over a year that the end result of Washington's spending binge will be a European-style value-added tax (VAT). And sure enough, just days after Obamacare became law, Obama economic adviser Paul Volcker said a VAT may be necessary to keep up with entitlement spending. After all, someone needs to pay for all of their big spending programs.

The much better way to restore confidence in America's economic future is for a new Congress to demonstrate a commitment to lowering the deficit without raising taxes by cutting discretionary spending rather than increasing it by 12 percent as Democrats proposed (before the president decided to freeze it at its new, much higher level).

Another, better way to create more jobs here at home *and* reduce our dependence on foreign oil is to remove unnecessary barriers to domestic energy production. No single source of energy will make us independent of the sheiks and autocrats who don't have our interests at heart. Republicans have developed a comprehensive strategy to develop new domestic sources of oil, gas, nuclear, shale from coal, wind, and solar. The Democrats' promises of magical new "green" jobs from shutting down domestic production of traditional energy sources are pie in the sky. In the past twenty years, Democrats on the national level became wedded to the ideology of the radical left—which looks at America's natural reserves and sees toxic waste sites. I believe that most Americans look at our energy reserves and see valuable natural resources that will help to ease drivers' pain at the pump and lessen our dependence on foreign oil. They understand that if we focus on developing all of our domestic sources, both traditional and renewable in environmentally secure ways, we can create jobs and increase our national security.

Speaking of jobs and economic growth, another critical area is education, a key driver for a more productive and vibrant workforce. In Virginia, this concern took the form of improving our schools and increasing access to education through helping families save for college. But Washington has a different role in education than the states and it has become too involved. These days, that role consists mainly of taking money from the states, bringing it to

Washington, and encouraging the earmarking and lobbying cultures that apportion education dollars according to muscle, not merit. Democrats can often be seen trying to allocate more and more federal tax dollars to our schools, and their intentions may be noble. Yet, despite the billions upon billions of federal dollars spent, achievement scores for American students are not where they need to be. Despite the fact that parents are constantly being taxed at the federal, state, and local levels, our children seem to be less and less equipped to compete with their foreign counterparts. Why? A big reason is because our dollars are going through lobbyists, middlemen, and bureaucrats before they ever reach our students and our classrooms. Considering America's more than 70 billion–dollar federal education budget, that's far too many dollars ending up away from our children.

So let's get education dollars out of Washington and back, closer to our communities. My colleague Joe Pitts of Pennsylvania has a "Dollars to the Classroom" bill that would require that 95 cents of every federal education dollar go to the classroom, not the bureaucracy and the special interests. This is a commonsense, twenty-first-century approach to education that would provide immediate benefits to our children. But, I believe we should go further. We can and should do the same with federal spending on transportation, housing, and other needs best left to the states and communities. The more Washington spends, the more bureaucracy and special interests are attracted like flies to the nation's capital to demand even more spending, perpetuating the cycle of big government.

Want to drain the swamp in Washington? Stop the culture of cronyism and keep more of those dollars on the local level.

———— ★ ————

On jobs, the economy, energy and education, Republicans have put forward real solutions over the past year and half. But there is no more egregious example of our ideas—as well as the opinions of the American people—being overlooked by the current Washington majority than fixing our health-care system.

From the passionate town hall meetings of the summer of 2009 to the concerned citizens who converged on the Capitol as the Democratic majority maneuvered and manipulated its plan into law in 2010, Americans have sent signal after signal to Washington that they're listening and they're engaged. They've been telling Washington that they understand that health-care reform will have a profound effect, not just on themselves, but on generations of Americans not yet born. Our children, grandchildren, and great-grandchildren will pay the price for government health care in jobs and wages lost, in higher taxes, and in rationed and diminished quality of care.

This is the message that America has been sending the powers that be in Washington DC for over a year now. And for over a year, Washington has refused to listen. Instead, Democrats wrote the bill in secret without allowing input from dissenting Democrats or Republicans. They coerced wavering members for their votes with smarmy sweetheart deals like the $300 million "Louisiana Purchase." They resorted to legislative trickery and arm-twisting when they couldn't get enough legitimate votes to pass their bill. They forced through a trillion dollar overhaul of one sixth of our economy literally in defiance of the people they represent.

Overwhelmingly, Americans believe in building upon what works in our health-care system so that they can continue to enjoy the best care in the world. This health-care bill does the opposite. It destroys the system it purports to save.

Paul, Kevin, and I agree with the need to take action on health care. We do not accept the status quo. That's why we are committed, not simply to repealing Democratic health-care reform, but replacing it with a system that works for all Americans by focusing first and foremost on lowering costs.

What does a health-care system that works for all Americans look like? Republicans believe in providing individuals and families with more affordable options without costly mandates by expanding insurance market competition. We would allow families to buy insurance across state lines and give every individual and small business the same access to tax incentives and pooling opportunities that unions and corporations have today. We would end discrimination against Americans with preexisting conditions by creating state-based high risk pools, not by forcing everyone to pay more. And we would do something the Democrats will never do: reduce health-care costs by taking on the trial lawyers who force physicians into defensive medicine, which drives up costs for everyone.

Just days after the Democratic health-care bill was signed into law, American companies began to announce the higher costs they will experience under the law—costs that will be passed on to their employees and their customers. Before America's competitiveness is reduced, our taxes raised, and our health-care system irreparably damaged, we need to repeal Democratic health-care reform and replace it with a better way. Paul, Kevin, and I are already on the job.

———— ★ ————

America's challenges at home are real and pressing. But the job of a leader is to keep his or her eye on the bigger picture. And whether our current leaders in Washington always remember or not, America has real enemies in the world—enemies who don't care if they're read their Miranda rights or get a civilian trial, just that they kill as many innocents as they can.

As an American Jew, I am acutely aware of the existence

of evil in the world. In 2006, my cousin, Daniel, was killed in a terrorist attack in Tel Aviv. I'll never forget when then-House Speaker Denny Hastert invited Daniel's family up from Florida to hear Israeli Prime Minister Ehud Olmert speak to a joint session of Congress. After the speech, I invited Daniel's family, along with two representatives from south Florida, Ileana Ros-Lehtinen and Debbie Wasserman Schultz, to my office for coffee. It was there that Daniel's father, Tuly, told us the story of his son's death for the first time.

He and Daniel had been sitting in a café in Tel Aviv, Tuly said, when the terrorist walked in with a backpack. As the security guard asked to search the terrorist's pack, Tuly watched as the terrorist detonated the bomb inside. The next thing Tuly knew, the power of the blast forced his son back into him. Daniel caught all the shrapnel and, in doing so, saved his father's life. By the time Tuly had finished, we were all in tears.

No one needs to tell me about the bad guys out there. But being an American Jew has also given me a unique perspective on the good guys. Unlike some in Washington today, I don't have any doubt about the moral strength of America. We have our flaws, it's true. But we're the good guys. We make mistakes, but we never set out to do evil or do harm to other people.

Contrary to what the conspiracy theorists say, America doesn't have any imperialist impulses; we're not out to conquer the world for power, oil, or any other trophy.

Unlike European colonial powers, America's museums aren't stocked with artifacts and works of art plundered from abroad. What we do have, though, is a set of beliefs. We believe in government by the consent of the governed. We believe in freedom of speech. We believe in full and equal rights for women. We believe in the economic freedom to work hard and see your work rewarded. We believe in the freedom to worship as you choose or not to worship at all. Make no mistake—it's these beliefs, not any real or imagined offense that America has committed—that our enemies resent.

Unlike some of our current leaders in Washington, I know we have real differences with our enemies, and that these differences can't be negotiated away. There is always a time and a place for diplomacy, of course. But I subscribe to the fundamental soundness of what the author Primo Levi said when he was asked what he learned from the Holocaust.

He said, "When a man with a gun says he's going to kill you—believe him."

Today, the head of state with the most dangerous gun pointed at the head of the United States is Mahmoud Ahmadinejad, the tyrant of Iran. Under Ahmadinejad and his cronies, in just the past year and a half Iran has stolen an election, brutally crushed a democracy movement, and, most seriously of all for the United States and our ally Israel, ramped up its effort to develop a nuclear program.

The stakes are too high for us not to recognize that

the policy of engagement with Tehran has failed. Ahma-dinejad has simply used the time spent in further, futile negotiations to bring his nuclear program closer to fruition. In just the time we have spent "reaching out" to Ahma-dinejad, secret Iranian nuclear enrichment sites have been discovered and Iranian officials have promised that there will soon be more. Even toothless United Nations nuclear inspectors have come around to believing that Iran's nuclear program isn't "peaceful," as Iranian officials have laughably claimed. It's not hard to see the writing on the wall. No matter how many times Secretary of State Hillary Clinton insists that the Obama administration views the Iranian development of nuclear weapons as "unacceptable," the unacceptable keeps happening. It's looking for all the world like this administration is preparing to accept the reality of a nuclear armed Iran.

In fairness, administrations of both parties have done little to stop Iran's march toward nuclear weapons, even as they have loudly complained about the "unacceptability" of it all. But the time for talk—even tough talk—is over. We would be lying to ourselves if we believed that a nuclear Iran could be deterred. A nuclear weapon in Ahmadinejad's hands will allow the world's most notorious state sponsor of terrorism to commit nuclear blackmail against whom-ever it pleases. It will pose an existential threat to the state of Israel, precipitate a full-fledged arms race in the Mid-dle East, and gravely damage the national security of the United States.

There is a better way to deal with the tyrant of Tehran. America has to treat Ahmadinejad and the Iranian regime like the thugs and agents of terror that they are, not like the trustworthy and compromising leaders we all wish they were. That means real sanctions, with real teeth. It means sending the message to the world that if you deal with Iran, you are not welcome to deal with the United States. It means empowering the brave Iranians who oppose the regime instead of leaving them to be shot on the street. And it means making sure Tehran understands that the option of force *is* on the table. We cannot and should not delude ourselves into thinking that Ahmadinejad will change course unless threatened with anything less.

As troubling as the Obama policy toward Iran is, it is of a piece with a larger double standard this administration has when dealing with the Middle East. The Obama administration's way of showing it's an honest broker in the Middle East peace process has been to overlook multiple offenses on the part of some in the Arab world while irresponsibly attacking Israel. This is a major policy shift, the ramifications of which will be very serious.

Last March, Vice President Biden made a much-publicized trip to Israel. While he was there, two separate incidents occurred that illustrate the administration's shocking double standard toward the Middle East. You may have heard of the first incident, but I doubt you've heard of the second, as it received very little coverage in the media.

In the first incident, a middle-level Israeli bureaucrat

announced the approval of sixteen hundred homes in an existing Jewish neighborhood in the Israeli capital of Jerusalem. The decision was a routine bureaucratic one, concerning a part of Israel that is not now nor has ever been in dispute. Israeli prime minister Benyamin Netanyahu immediately apologized for the clumsy timing of the announcement. Nonetheless, the Obama administration responded with suspiciously well-orchestrated outrage. Administration officials took to the network news shows to call the announcement an "affront." Secretary of State Hillary Clinton spent forty-five minutes on the phone with Prime Minister Netanyahu reprimanding him for sending "a deeply negative signal about Israel's approach to the bilateral [U.S.-Israel] relationship." The administration's disproportionate reaction to the Israeli bureaucracy's act of paper pushing sent our relations with Israel to a new low.

Now consider the second incident, which also occurred during Vice President Biden's trip to Israel in March. On one of the last days of the vice president's visit, Palestinian president Mahmoud Abbas' Fatah party held a ceremony dedicating a public square in Ramallah to Dalal Mughrabi. In 1978, Mughrabi led the bloodiest terror attack in Israel's history. She and her confederates attacked a bus full of civilians on an outing, killing 38 Israelis, including 13 children, and an American photojournalist. During the ceremony, Fatah representatives unveiled a statue in Mughrabi's honor and hailed her as a hero. "We are all Dalal Mughrabi," a senior Fatah official told *The New York Times*. "For us she is not a terrorist" but "a fighter who fought for the liberation of her own land."

The administration's response to this outrage? Not a word.

From the president's much-hyped speech to the world's Muslims in Cairo to repeated provocations of Israel, the current administration's goal has been to ingratiate itself with the Arab world at the expense of our best friend in the Middle East. This strategy makes a kind of twisted sense for an administration that equates currying favor with international elites with advancing the national security interests of the country. But what has this kid gloves treatment of the world's despots gotten us? North Korea and Iran continue to seek nuclear weapons capabilities. When Russia isn't helping them, it is backsliding into authoritarianism. And Al-Qaeda seems unconvinced by the administration's promises to close the detention facility at Guantánamo Bay. It keeps sending suicide bombers—including one last Christmas day—to kill innocent Americans.

Our leaders need to recognize who our enemies are and remember who our friends are. America stands with Israel for both moral and strategic reasons. Israel is not only a democratic ally and our only true friend in the Middle East; it is also a vital pillar of U.S. national security strategy. When it is strong—its borders secure, its people free from the threat of Iran and its terrorist proxies—the Middle East is a much more stable and peaceful place.

On the other hand, if Iran and the terrorist organizations Hamas and Hezbollah are allowed to grow stronger at Israel's expense, the resulting victory for radical forces would deal a blow to U.S. antiterrorism efforts. Terrorism gains legitimacy and momentum when it is shown to work.

Instead, we must demand that the Palestinians stamp out anti-Israel incitement and stop dragging their feet on fighting homegrown terrorism. And we also ought to insist that Egypt, Saudi Arabia, and Jordan move the Arab world toward a normalization of relations with Israel. If the administration's goal is to ingratiate itself with the Arab world at the expense of our democratic ally Israel, perhaps it has achieved mild success. But if its goal is to hasten the peace process and shore up a united front against terrorism and a nuclear Iran, the administration has lurched in the opposite direction and put our national security interests in jeopardy.

House Republicans have also offered better solutions for keeping America safe from terrorists here at home. From day one, the Obama administration has been hell bent on closing the terrorist detention facility at Guantánamo Bay—without any idea what it will do with the dangerous men being held there. It was a policy without a solution, a bone for the liberal base, and a dangerous position for a new commander in chief to take on the world stage.

And their crusade to close Gitmo was just the opening act in their strategy of transforming the military safeguards that had kept America safe since 9/11 into a bad episode of *Law & Order*.

From giving terrorist masterminds civilian trials in

New York City to reading the Christmas 2009 "underwear bomber" his rights after fifty minutes of interrogation to suggesting that the Times Square bomber was motivated by his mortgage problems, the Democrats in charge in Washington have revealed a fundamental failure to understand the enemy we face. The mechanics of our civilian law enforcement system, with its defense attorneys, discovery rights, and admirable openness, are designed fundamentally to respond to crimes; to react when a wrong has been committed. Terrorism represents a fundamentally different kind of danger. We can't afford to wait for terrorists to strike and then use our civilian system to react. Our leaders owe us more than making sure the perpetrators are caught and tried in the aftermath of a terrorist attack that leaves thousands of Americans dead. They owe us the protection of these American lives from terrorism in the first place. In overlooking this, the Obama administration has shown itself to be disconnected, not just from the most effective ways to keep America safe, but from the American people themselves.

President Obama deserves credit for not following up on his campaign promise and recklessly leaving Iraq to slide back into chaos and terror. And while we wish he did not put a timetable for his surge in Afghanistan, the president also deserves credit and our thanks for doubling down on our efforts to defeat the Taliban in Afghanistan. Preventing both these countries from becoming safe harbors for terrorists is critical to our safety and security.

Still, the president and his advisers seem more driven by the opinions of the global elite than the American people when it comes to dealing with individual terrorists here at home. For so many of us, our first thoughts the morning of September 11, 2001, were, "Is my family safe? Do I have a friend at work in the Pentagon this morning? What about lower Manhattan?"

Our leaders in Washington may have moved on from this overriding concern, but we have not. Americans want solutions to keep our country safe. And the applause of international elites? That we can live without.

———— ★ ————

The stakes of what has been involved in the debate we've been having in this country over the past eighteen months came home to me in a shocking way in the waning days of the health-care debate. It was then that the FBI informed me that a man in Philadelphia had posted a video online threatening to kill me and my family.

I am deeply grateful that law enforcement officials found this man and arrested him before he could do any harm to my family or myself. Following the health-care debate, I spoke out forcefully against, not just extremists, but the activists and media who used acts and threats by extremists to advance their political agenda. There is unequivocally no place for violence or threats of violence in a nation governed by the consent of the governed.

But the exploitation of these threats following the health-care debate did a great harm to the America people: it served as a distraction from the great majority of peaceful, democratic Americans who are deeply upset and yes, even angry, about government health-care reform and the way it was passed.

Sadly, I believe that for some activists and mainstream journalists, this distraction was deliberate. Their goal was to paint every American who disagrees with the president and the Democratic majority as violent extremists, even racists. But calling your fellow American a racist, a proto-Nazi, or a bigot is just about the worst thing you can say about someone in today's society. This isn't just overheated rhetoric. It's is a vicious affront to decent, law-abiding, and dissenting Americans.

Beginning even before this administration came into office, Americans have had a growing feeling that the game is rigged against them in Washington. Politicians of both parties have ruled like machine bosses, cutting deals for favored groups, bailing out corporate cronies, and disregarding the voices and the concerns of the American people. While millions of Americans are out of work and struggling, Washington's answers have been bridges to nowhere, corporate cronyism, cap and trade, housing bailouts, and government-run health care. Hardworking Americans don't feel like the playing field is level; they don't think they have a fair shot anymore. When they're not feeling condescended to, American are feeling shut out of the process. Washington has some hard work to do. You will see in the coming chapters how Paul, Kevin, and I have a plan for winning in November and tackling the tough choices we're going to have to make to preserve the greatness of America for future generations.

America is at a crossroads. We have real challenges and Americans are looking for solutions. But we believe in the wisdom and decency of the men and women who put us here. Americans have encountered rough times in the past, and we've always emerged stronger than before. What our country needs today is leadership to see us through the tough choices ahead—responsible, adult leadership that listens to and respects the American people.

The current majority in Congress has refused to listen to the people. But Paul, Kevin, and I have a message for our fellow Americans: we hear you. We hear you loud and clear.

PART TWO

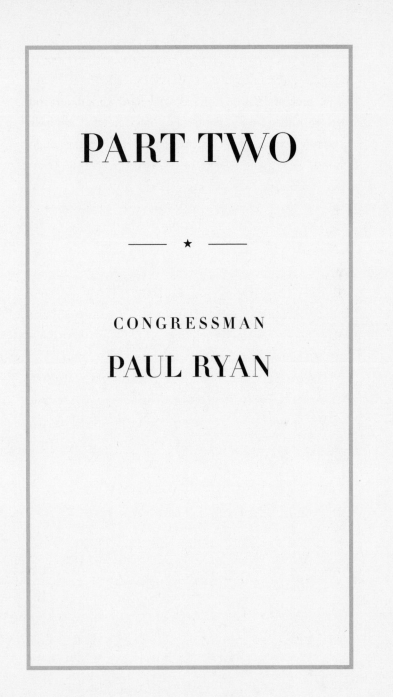

★

CONGRESSMAN
PAUL RYAN

CHAPTER FOUR

Health-Care Reform and the New Way in Washington

———— ★ ————

I t was my fortieth birthday.

The President of the United States was talking to me.

And here's the kicker: he was *complimenting* me, my family, and my ideas.

It happened in Baltimore, early in 2010, at the House Republicans yearly, members-only get together. When we were planning the meeting, we decided to do something different. We invited President Obama to come and talk to us—not something opposing parties usually do. But then the president, to his credit, did something different, too. He accepted.

So President Obama comes to our retreat and we have a substantive exchange about our different visions for spurring job growth and reforming our health-care system.

Then we have lunch. And as I'm sitting there, surrounded by my family and other House Republicans, with my six-year-old son on my knee, the president picks me out of the crowd and starts talking to me. Just days before, I had released my Roadmap for America's Future, a detailed blueprint for how we can bring spending under control, secure the future of Social Security and Medicare, and reclaim the American idea. We had been sparring, civilly but seriously, with the president about many of the challenges addressed in the Roadmap, so when the president singled me out, I expected to be barraged with criticism. Instead, I was showered with compliments.

President Obama called my Roadmap "a serious proposal." He called me a "pretty sincere guy." He even said I have a "beautiful family." It seemed too good to last.

It was.

It took less than seventy-two hours for the president's budget director, Peter Orszag, to attack my plan as a risky scheme. Democrats circulated a so-called "fact sheet" peppered liberally with fighting words like "privatize" and tired hits against President Bush. They charged that my plan was a tax cut for the rich, which would expose seniors to "greater risks and/or lower-quality coverage." And then, just to be sure they got their point across, Democratic House members held a conference call with the media to hyperventilate that Roadmap supporters are "frozen in the ice of their own indifference." I'm not making this up.

There is something about the alternative vision I put

forth that must have really gotten under their skin. In fact, my plan was the polar opposite of what the Democrats were charging it was, and I think they knew that. Far from "gutting" entitlement programs for retirees and the needy, my plan would save these programs from looming bankruptcy. But too often in Washington you can judge the veracity of a political argument by its decibel level: the less substantive the talking points, the louder they are shouted. And Democrats were screaming at the top of their lungs.

———— ★ ————

As I look back on it, the coordinated effort to change the subject from their budget-busting policies and to demagogue an alternative that actually tackles the fiscal crisis they're accelerating makes sense. It fits the pattern of the way public policy—particularly health-care reform—has been "debated" in Washington over the past eighteen months.

All of us learned in grade school (and from watching *Schoolhouse Rock!*) the way a bill becomes a law. It starts with an open debate. There is opportunity for bipartisan input. Then there is an up or down vote in both houses— the House and the Senate—on the merits of the bill. Then, if the House and Senate bills are not absolutely identical, there is a conference with members from both houses to reach a compromise that will satisfy both. This is followed by what is usually a final vote in the House and Senate on the "reconciled" bill. Then—and only then—does the president sign the measure into law. Sure, there's always been some level of horse-trading and deal-making, but the Constitution sets out this process as the method by which the people govern themselves in America through their elected representatives, and that process has generally been faithfully adhered to. That's the regular American way of our national democracy.

But business in Washington these days isn't being conducted the way our Founders envisioned—and certainly not in a manner that respects the consent of the governed. We have seen over the past two years a new Washington Way, raised from the depths to new heights of political corruption in the health-care debacle.

This new Washington Way isn't open debate broadcast on C-SPAN; it's closed-door, backroom deals. The Washington Way doesn't seek input from both sides of the issue; it muscles through bills on strict one-party votes. And the Washington Way isn't interested in honest up-or-down votes on transformational programs. It rigs the process to produce the outcome it desires through any means necessary. The ends justify the means. Bend the Constitution to keep up with the change.

In short, the defining feature of the new Washington Way is that it strips the power of making law away from the people, whose consent is the basis for our democracy. The new Washington Way is designed to transfer lawmaking to a small elite group who know what is best for us. And from start to finish, the way President Obama and the Democratic majority went about supposedly fixing our health-care system has been conducted in the new Washington Way.

The American people were cut out of the Democrats' health-care reform vision from the beginning. Remember the Emmanuel Doctrine: "Never let a serious crisis go to waste"? From the outset, the Democratic strategy was to use a national crisis—the financial meltdown—as an excuse to pass their version of government-driven health-care reform. The treacherous plan was to exploit Americans' sense of urgency about jobs and the economy to sneak through an unrelated government entitlement. That strategy could hardly be more antidemocratic.

But then the majority party encountered a roadblock: the more Americans learned about their health-care reform plan, the less they liked it. So supporters made the strategic decision to create an inverse relationship between the public's support for the policy and its input in the plan's formulation. As opposition to Obamacare escalated, the American people were more and more shut out of the legislative process.

The initial goal was to pass the bill before the August recess. But when that deadline wasn't met, tens of thousands of Americans got the opportunity to express their opposition to the bill when members went back to their districts for town hall meetings. Suddenly, news reports and

YouTube were full of videos of angry citizens confronting often dazed and defensive members of Congress. Immediately after that, the president and a small number of advisers and Democratic leaders retreated behind closed doors to write their health-care bill. They didn't like what they were hearing from Americans, so they told us, in no uncertain terms, to shut up and sit down.

But the American people refused to be silenced. Next, voters in Virginia and New Jersey showed their displeasure with Democratic government in the 2009 off-year elections by electing committed pro-market, limited government candidates. The candidates who had run as supporters of the big government, Democratic agenda lost, and the message was not lost on lawmakers in Washington DC. The price of passing the increasingly unpopular health-care bill got higher. So the White House, along with House Speaker Nancy Pelosi and Senate Majority Leader Harry Reid, resorted to bribing skittish Democratic lawmakers. Thus were born the "Louisiana Purchase," in which $300 million in extra Medicaid funding was given to Louisiana to secure the vote of a senator from that state; the "Cornhusker Kickback," in which the taxpayers permanently picked up the tab for the expansion of Medicaid in Nebraska—and Nebraska alone—to buy off a Nebraska lawmaker; and "Gator Aid," in which 800,000 Florida seniors were exempted from Obamacare's cuts to Medicare in order to win the support of a senator from Florida. And that, we know now, is just a partial list.

And with every new backroom bribe, Americans intuitively understood that if legislation had to be passed through a series of corrupt deals with alliterative names, it was neither worthwhile on its own terms nor legitimate by democratic standards. The Republicans' "Bridge to Nowhere" once rightly disgusted the American people. Now the Democrats' string of constitutionally suspect sweetheart deals was making all previous corruption look amateurish.

And then, last but certainly not least, came the health-care reform endgame earlier in 2010. Voters in Massachusetts had dealt what many believed at the time was the death blow to Democratic health-care reform when they elected Sen. Scott Brown (R) in January to fill the seat of the Senate's premier advocate of a government-driven health-care program, the late Sen. Ted Kennedy.

Scott Brown's victory in Massachusetts had made passing Democratic health-care reform through the democratic process impossible. In the campaign, Brown had promised the voters of Massachusetts he would be the forty-first vote in the Senate against Obamacare and they took him up on his offer. Without the sixty votes necessary for a filibuster-proof majority to pass their version of health-care reform, the majority party became desperate.

The only way left was the new Washington Way. If supporters of government health care couldn't summon the votes necessary to pass health-care reform through the democratic process, they would just bypass the democratic process. Self-government stands or falls on integrity, not only in those who represent you but in the enactment of law.

In the Senate, that meant employing what Progressivists and their friends in the mainstream media had called the "nuclear option" when Republicans considered it, but was now, in the gentle hands of Democrats, deemed a simple "up or down vote." This process, known as budget reconciliation, requires only a simple majority of fifty-one votes to pass a bill. It was created to align spending and tax laws with the levels spelled out in the budget. Over time, it came to be used mainly to reduce budget deficits or, more broadly, to limit the growth of government. It had never been used—never—to push through a $1,000,000,000,000 expansion of government and to seize control of one-sixth of the economy.

In the House, a process called "deem and pass" was essentially the same thing: legislative trickery to enact legislation that does not have majority backing. It meant that the House would pass the 2,700-page health-care bill without *ever actually voting for it.* House Speaker Nancy Pelosi said it all when she said, in the final days of the debate, "But we have to pass the bill so that you can find out what is in it."

Let me say that again: the Democratic leader in the House was telling the American people that they would pass the bill first, and we could ask questions later. This was the government "transparency" that President Obama had promised? The arrogance, the paternalism, and the condescension marking the Democratic leadership's radical method for getting health-care reform through were breathtaking in their repudiation of popular consent and the implications for the future of popular government under the current leadership.

Public outrage and the protests of both Republican and Democratic members compelled Speaker Pelosi to back away from the "deem and pass" strategy of passing the bill without actually voting on it. The ugly health-care debacle finally came to an end with final passage of the overhaul in the House on March 21, 2010—signed into law two days later. The Left in Washington celebrated what they called the "third wave" of big government progressivism. Two hundred and nineteen House Democrats voted for the bill, thirty-four opposed it. No Republican, in the House or the Senate, voted for the bill. For the first time since before the Civil War, the minority party was so completely excluded from the shaping of major reform legislation that it voted unanimously against the final bill.

———— ★ ————

The convoluted legislative charade by Democratic supporters of government health care last spring demonstrates how far the Democratic majority has wandered from real health-care reform and cost control. They had come to the point where the debate was no longer about doing what was best for the American people. It was about winning at any cost.

And that's unfortunate, because there are real problems in health care waiting to be fixed. President Obama was right when he argued that to get a grip on our exploding debts we need to rein in health-care costs. The problem is, he and his allies immediately jumped to the mistaken conclusion that health-care spending can be brought under control if you make *government* do the spending.

Getting a grip on health-care costs is both a budgetary necessity and a moral imperative. It will not only save our country from bankruptcy, it will expand access to health care, and avoid saddling our children and grandchildren with unbearable debt. But the inescapable truth of Obamacare is that it fails to address this central problem of skyrocketing health-care costs. The independent, nonpartisan Congressional Budget Office estimates that families' premiums could rise 10–13 percent under government health care. Private sector analysts put that number even higher.

The higher costs to American families under the Democratic health-care overhaul are driven by this fact: even though it doesn't contain the so-called "public option," Obamacare is still a government takeover of our health-care system. This is not reform that drives costs lower through choice and competition. It is reform that drives costs higher through centralizing resources and decision-making in Washington DC.

The premise of the Democratic system is that because everything is connected to everything else, government must ultimately control everything. It assumes that you can provide coverage for pre-existing conditions only if you have healthy people in the insurance pool to spread costs. Of course, to get young and healthy people into the system, you have to mandate that everyone buy insurance. But to do this, you have to subsidize people who can't afford insurance and penalize those employers who don't provide insurance. And once you start handing out subsidies and penalties, you give more and more people an incentive to join the system. Costs rise, and to slow their rise you have to impose limits on care by stripping decision-making power from patients and doctors.

The entire architecture of Democratic health care is designed to give the federal government control over what kind of insurance is available for patients, how much health care is enough, and which treatments are worth it for government to pay for.

In addition to setting the price, the Obama plan empowers Washington to determine the kind of insurance that will be available. It gives the secretary of Health and Human Services and an unelected group of federal bureaucrats—a new Health Benefits Advisory Committee— unprecedented power to determine what constitutes "acceptable coverage."

It gives the U.S. Preventive Services Task Force new powers to further limit patient choice, allowing the secretary of Health and Human Services to unilaterally deny payment for prevention services contrary to Task Force recommendations.

It empowers a "comparative effectiveness board," created by last year's "stimulus" bill that will restrict providers' decisions about what treatments are best for their patients.

In the end, Democrats tried to argue that their plan will not only solve rising health-care costs, it will reduce the budget as well. They manipulated government accountants at the Congressional Budget Office (CBO) in an attempt to make the laughable claim that they—not opponents of Obamacare—are the fiscally responsible ones.

But as Ronald Reagan used to say, you are entitled to your own opinions but not your own facts. And the fact is that when all spending is counted, CBO concludes that the Democratic health-care reform will increase health-care costs, not decrease them. Premiums for individuals will increase and costs for middle-class families will rise. Costs will rise even further by the increase in demand created by the law accompanied by the decrease in supply it will create. President Obama's own Medicare actuary has estimated that about 15 percent of providers who rely on Medicare could leave the system under the plan.

And as for the Democrats' claim of deficit reduction, it is about as trustworthy as their promise to cut health-care costs. Their health-care program will cost an astounding $2.6 trillion in its first full decade after the spending is fully implemented. And to make matters worse, the Democrats deceitfully kick the can down the road when it comes to paying this enormous bill. Their plan leaves it to another president and another Congress to tax so-called "Cadillac" plans in 2018. Even more egregious, it contains a promise— a promise that Democrats were implicitly breaking even as they made it—to make $208 billion in future cuts to physician pay under Medicare. No one—and I mean no one— believed Congress would ever make such a cut. As writer Yuval Levin put it, "This is not fiscal responsibility; it's not even naïveté or self-delusion. It's just dishonesty."

One of my heroes, the economist Milton Friedman, used to have a saying: "There's no such thing as a free lunch." What he meant is that nothing is free; someone, somewhere, always pays. Despite utopian marketing promises, government health care is not exempt from Friedman's dictum. Far from it. It will raise costs, and someone, somewhere, will pay. By creating a new health-care entitlement while doing nothing to restrain health-care costs, let alone the needless overuse of medical facilities, Democratic health reform will inevitably lead to rationing of care and higher costs. There is no "free" health care just like there is no free lunch. Someone always pays. The American people understand without having to be told that this "someone" is them.

★

Of all the many misfortunes of the health-care debate, the greatest is that, from the beginning, there was a better way.

From the very beginning of the debate, Republicans and Democrats have put forward responsible health-care reform proposals that empower consumers—patients—instead of government. Proposals that slow the growth of health-care spending by inviting true choice and competition into the health care market—all while preserving a safety net for those Americans who truly need it.

At the onset of the debate, I joined with several colleagues in the House and Senate in offering The Patients' Choice Act—a comprehensive reform proposal that provide access to quality, affordable coverage for all Americans. It starts by ending the tax discrimination against people who don't get health insurance from their employer. Every respected economist—and every honest politician—knows that the tax exclusion for employer-provided health-coverage subsidizes insurance companies instead of health care, hides the true cost of coverage, and disproportionately favors the wealthy at the expense of the self-employed, the unemployed, and small businesses. The Patients' Choice Act replaces the bias in the tax code with universal tax credits so that all Americans have the resources to purchase portable, affordable coverage that best suits their needs, with additional support provided for those with lower incomes.

Through a combination of tax credits, high-risk pools, transparency, regulatory reform, and information technology, patient-centered reforms would foster a vibrant health-care marketplace. In stark contrast to the plan passed by the majority in Congress, my plan unapologetically seeks to apply our nation's timeless principles—our Founders' commitment to individual liberty, limited government, and free enterprise—to today's challenges. It does so in a way that honors our historic commitment to strengthening the social safety net for those who need it most.

In stark contrast to the Democrats' 2,700-page monstrosity, House Republicans put forward a number of commonsense alternatives focused on addressing the fundamental problem of costs. Republicans offered solutions allowing consumers to buy health insurance across state lines with an eye to the product and the price that is best for the individual consumer. House Republicans put forward what Democrats dare not do lest they jeopardize their number one source of campaign funding: it ends the gravy train of medical malpractice lawsuits for the trial lawyers. House Republicans set out a series of substantive but incremental steps that could be agreed to by bipartisan majorities. It fixes what is broken in our health-care system without breaking what is working.

All of these proposals were deliberately ignored by President Obama and the Democratic majority that controls Congress because they didn't fit with their government-driven plan. In retrospect, it's clear that the last year's debate wasn't about health care at all. It wasn't about how to get a grip on costs, make quality care more accessible, put patients back in control, or even how to address exclusions for preexisting conditions.

Instead, this was a debate about changing America. From the crude attacks on alternative visions like my Roadmap, to the gutter politics of the new Washington Way, the last year and a half has been about a group of men and women exploiting a crisis and seizing their moment to redefine the relationship between Americans and their government.

The weekend in March that the House voted on the health-care bill, thousands of Americans swarmed the Capitol, waving signs and making their voices heard. Every hour, one hundred thousand calls came in from across the country. The reason? Washington Democrats weren't just in the process of changing America, they were in the process of changing the life of every American. Because in the end, health care isn't about budgets and balance sheets, it's about your life and your family's lives, and how best to protect them. It's the most intimate, most deeply personal part of our public policy. And there we were, debating whether the government—in the form of unelected bureaucrats in Washington DC—should have a bigger role in our most personal decisions.

This entire episode represented a tragic missed opportunity to tackle the fundamental problems in health care. Skyrocketing costs are driving more and more families and businesses to the brink of bankruptcy, leaving affordable coverage out of reach for millions of Americans, and accelerating our path to fiscal ruin. This is the central challenge, and yet the congressional majority went about addressing it backward. They used the force of government to cover all Americans, and now they will have to figure out which screws to twist to contain costs. They went for this approach because their concern was never about costs. It was about expanding coverage through an expansion of government.

A bill may have passed, but the challenge of how to deal with the seemingly inexorable increase of health-care costs is one from which Eric, Kevin, and I will not shrink. We intend to continue advancing true patient-centered reforms like attaching tax benefits to the individual rather than the job, breaking down barriers to interstate competition, and promoting transparency and consumer-friendly coverage options.

We will continue to fight to ensure that health-care decisions are made by patients and their doctors, not by bureaucrats, whether at an insurance company or a government agency. By inviting market forces into health care, we can encourage a system where doctors, insurers, and hospitals compete against one another for the business of informed consumers.

We will continue this fight because it is a fight about the idea of America. Americans aren't any particular nationality. And America isn't just a landmass from Hawaii to Maine to Wisconsin to Florida. America is an idea. It's the most pro-human idea ever conceived of by man—

the idea that our rights come from our Creator, not from government.

Americans today are being asked to subscribe to an ideology that is against the American idea. It's an ideology that says that government creates rights—and government takes them away. This ideology rejects the goal of government as securing equal opportunity, it demands that government create equal results. It is an ideology that treats citizens like children and politicians like divinities. It is not an ideology that need prevail in American life. Not on our watch.

We can take being the Democrats' whipping boys. We can take the attacks. What we can't take is losing the timeless ideas that made this country history's greatest experiment in freedom—and that will endure as long as Americans keep faith with those ideas.

CHAPTER FIVE

The Tipping Point

———— ★ ————

Before I came to Congress I spent some time at what Washington self-approvingly calls a "think tank." I wrote speeches about the economy for true conservative heroes like Jack Kemp and Bill Bennett at Empower America. For the past four years in the House of Representatives, I've been the leading Republican on the Budget Committee. So I've looked at the numbers. And for as long as I have been studying the amount of tax dollars spent by the federal government versus the amount of revenue it takes in, it has been painfully clear that America is on an unsustainable fiscal path.

We're rapidly approaching a point of no return; a tipping point after which we become a country most Americans have never dreamed we would be. If we keep spending like we're spending, America will become a place where unprecedented levels of debt overwhelm the budget, smother the economy, weaken our competitiveness in the twenty-first-century global economy, and threaten the survival of programs for the truly needy. Worse yet, we will become a culture in which self-reliance becomes a vice and dependency a virtue; a place where so many Americans are dependent upon government that our country comes to reject individual initiative, entrepreneurship, and opportunity that made us great.

As Eric has already written, too much of our recent political history has been spent trading accusations about which political party cares about the American people more than the other. There's been seemingly constant competition to brand one party the party that's in it for the people and the other party the party that's in it for themselves. As usual, Washington has been treating the American people like children, not talking about substantive differences, just calling each other names. My party: good. Your party: bad.

But this argument—whoever makes it, Democrat or Republican—is a distraction. I truly believe that most Americans regardless of party agree that the status quo is unacceptable. Republican and Democratic partisans both know that Americans are hurting. We know that too many Americans are out of work or in grim fear of losing their jobs. We know that health-care costs are out of control. They're bankrupting our small businesses, they're bankrupting families, and they're bankrupting our government.

The fundamental difference in American politics today

isn't about who cares the most, it's about which party is committed to the ideas and principles that have never failed in the past to solve our nation's problems while preserving individual freedom and equal opportunity. And here, we don't agree with the party that currently dominates Washington. We have real differences. In fact, Washington's self-proclaimed Progressives see the crisis in spending and debt coming just as clearly as we do. The difference is, they're not interested in applying the brakes. They *want* to see America hurtle past the point of no return. They welcome the level of government spending and the level of government control in our lives that's necessary for a European-style welfare state. Their paternalistic philosophy calls for a self-reinforcing expansion of government. This isn't just a narrow political ploy on their part, although an ever-growing population dependent on government is good for the party of government. In advocating government-controlled health care and a national energy tax, Progressives are showing the zeal of their ideological convictions. They truly *believe* the best course for America is to abandon the American idea for a model much like the European Union.

We believe these latter-day Progressives could not be more mistaken, about both the meaning of America and the passion of Americans for the idea that still makes this nation an exception in the world.

The result is that today America is faced with a choice of two futures, a choice that has rarely before been so clear and so consequential.

Think of this choice in terms of your own family. Imagine your family's future if you spent and borrowed like Washington does today and like Progressivists want to accelerate in the future. You'd owe $60 in credit card loans for every $100 of income. Every month you'd pay back a little but borrow even more. In ten years, you'll owe $87 for every $100 you make. Eventually, you have no choice but to hand off your debt to your kids. If they worked until 2035, they'd owe more than $180 for every $100 they earned. In 2050, your grandkids will owe more than $320 for every $100 they make. By 2080 they will owe seven times their earnings. Of course, the world's loan windows would slam shut long before then, but this is the path our government is on right now—the one Washington Progressives want us to go down even faster. It is the path to financial ruin and corrupted national character. It is choice number one.

Choice number two is a very different future. Imagine your family working, paying its bills, and enjoying a government that respects your work by allowing you to keep more of what you earn. If you're out of work, dynamic, results-based job training is available. As you look toward retirement, you know that a preserved and strengthened Social Security will be there, as well as your own safe and secure personal investments. Access to quality health coverage is universal and affordable because you and your family are at the center of a competitive, market-based system. If you lose your income because times get tough, a safety net is there to provide health care for you and your family. But at the end of the day, you have this confidence: you can reach high and provide a better life for your children and grandchildren because government hasn't taken the optimism and opportunity of America and turned it into stagnation or outright decline.

This is the choice that faces every American in 2010 and in the years to come. Some critics portray this as a choice between government and no government; between a life of safety and security in the nanny state and a nasty, brutish, and short life in a Hobbesian state of nature. In doing so, they employ raw fear in order to persuade us to accept a powerful Leviathan state as the only answer to our fear of the unknown future.

But the American people aren't children, and the choice before us isn't one of security versus insecurity, or safety versus fear. We are offering Americans the same choice as Ronald Reagan did more than a quarter century ago when he said: "It is not my intention to do away with government. It is, rather, to make it work—work with us, not over us; to stand by our side, not ride on our back. Government can and must provide opportunity, not smother it; foster productivity, not stifle it."

This fundamental choice has been debated in the name of many different things over the past year and a half: health-care reform, energy policy, economic policy, housing policy. But ultimately it's a debate about what kind of country we want to have.

———— ★ ————

What exactly do I mean when I say America is approaching a "tipping point"? In terms of the American political economy, I mean the point at which a critical mass of Americans receives more in government benefits than they pay in taxes.

Today, America is perilously close to this point. According to the Tax Foundation, 60 percent of Americans already receive more in benefits and services from the government than they pay in taxes. That means 60 percent of Americans don't bear the cost of the government they receive, so they don't have any incentive not to demand bigger government. Don't get me wrong. I'm all for the lowest taxes possible on the American people. But democracy itself becomes dangerously corrupted when the majority of people contribute little or nothing to pay for expanded government. The answer isn't for Americans to pay more taxes, but for government to be limited, and for all Americans to keep more of what they earn.

But in addition to the fiscal tipping point toward which we're hurtling, there is an even more important cultural transformation that America is approaching. Growing dependence on government threatens to transform the fundamental character of our country away from a culture of initiative and independence.

We've already seen this happen in many Western European countries. There, dependence on the government for their livelihoods turns into a complacency that has been described as soft despotism, where the benefits granted by government become far more important to most people than the precious right and power to govern themselves as individuals and as a society. Individuals become more timid, more worried about their securities than their liberties, more concerned to receive their government benefits than get ahead and make the most of their lives. The result is that these countries have high rates of taxation and persistent unemployment, coupled with low rates of productivity and growth. The Joint Economic Committee looked at twenty-three industrialized countries and found that countries with government spending in excess of 40 percent of GDP had half the average rate of economic growth as countries with less government. They may have government-mandated two-month vacations, but they have the high taxes and the high unemployment rates to match.

But that can't happen in America, right? Wrong. It *is* happening. Even though we don't yet have the kind of welfare state they have in Europe, our spending on entitlement programs like Social Security, Medicare, and Medicaid is on an unsustainable path. These programs are sacred trusts that we've made with elderly and poor Americans. But their very existence is threatened by a demographic wave that we know is coming. As the baby boomers grow older and retire, millions more will be added to the rolls of these entitlement programs. Americans are used to politicians talking about this coming crisis and then doing absolutely nothing about it. But we no longer have the luxury of kicking the can down the road. And thanks to the gusher of spending that has occurred in Washington over the past year and a half, we have even less time than before to save these programs.

The main drivers of our deepening deficits are the two major government health-care programs, Medicare and Medicaid. Together, they consume 22 percent of the federal budget—more than national defense, including the costs of the two wars. The problem is most acute in Medicare. Like Social Security, Medicare faces the daunting demographic challenge of supporting the baby boomers as they retire. But its much larger problem is that of medical costs, which are rising at roughly double the rate of growth in the economy. Today Medicare has an unfunded liability—or a deficit of projected revenues under projected costs—of $38 trillion over the next seventy-five years. This means that the federal government would have to set aside $38 trillion today to cover future benefits for the three generations of Americans: retirees, workers, and children. This translates to a burden of about $335,350 per U.S. household.

But that's just the beginning of the bad news. Because of ever-increasing numbers of new beneficiaries, skyrocketing health-care costs, and recently enacted health-care overhaul that will drive costs up, not down, this burden on American families will worsen rapidly. By 2014, Medicare's unfunded liability is projected to grow to $52 trillion, or about $458,900 per household.

Meanwhile, Social Security has gone bankrupt ahead of schedule. The same week in March that President Obama signed into law a new multitrillion dollar health-care entitlement, the Congressional Budget Office announced that in 2010 Social Security will pay out more in benefits than it receives in taxes. Social Security had been expected to hit this breaking point in 2016, but the recession is putting America's spiral into the red ahead of schedule. At this rate, in order to keep the program solvent, government will face the seemingly untenable choice of either cutting Social Security benefits nearly 25 percent or raising payroll taxes more than 30 percent.

When Social Security and Medicare are taken together, our total unfunded entitlement liability is $43 trillion, or about $379,475 for each and every American household.

In five years, that total will grow to $57 trillion, or over a half a million dollars—$500,414—per American family, rich or poor.

Taxes could be raised to pay for this massive spending. But our economy cannot withstand the levels of taxation necessary to finance this level of spending. The Congressional Budget Office found that by 2080, income tax rates (individual and corporate rates) would have to more than double to fund the projected spending path. Specifically, the current 10-percent income tax bracket would rise to 25 percent, and the current middle bracket of 25 percent would have to increase to 63 percent. The current top rate of 35 percent would rise to 88 percent. For the average family of four, that means a more than doubling of their income tax, from $3,100 today to $7,750—and this increase doesn't even include payroll taxes. The CBO provided these numbers *before* our cataclysmic recession, before Washington's reckless spending spree, and before the massive health-care budget buster.

The other option, if we don't change course, is to borrow the money we need. But as government borrows more, less capital is available for more productive private-sector investment. The United States already relies on foreign investors like China to finance about half of our debt. And as this debt rises, these investors will come to realize that the path of the deficit is unsustainable. The likely result is that they will reduce their purchases of U.S. securities (our debt), which will cause the dollar to be worth less on the international market. With the dollar worth less, lenders will raise interest rates to compensate, and the higher cost of borrowing will put upward pressure on consumer prices. This combination of high-interest rates and inflation will lower business profits and crash the stock market.

But more importantly, the standard of living of individual Americans will suffer devastating consequences. Our children—Americans born today—will face fewer jobs and stagnant incomes as they complete college and enter the workplace. By 2050, workers and families will begin seeing an erosion of their wages and incomes. By 2058, the economy will enter a free fall. Beyond that point, economists can't measure the impact on standards of living because the debt rises to levels the economy simply can't support.

———— ★ ————

Let me pause here to note that what I've already said about America's unsustainable fiscal path was true *before* the spending binge of the last year and a half. Our day of reckoning was always coming. President Obama and Democratic leaders in Washington are just seeing that it comes much sooner. In fact, they welcome this day of reckoning because they believe that from it will emerge a very different country from the one we've known.

Most of us grew up in an America in which hard work was rewarded and slacking off was penalized. When I was a kid in Janesville, Wisconsin, I learned early about the power of incentives. For just one B on my report card, my parents cut my allowance from $4 to $2. If I got a C, I got no allowance at all. Later, studying economics in college, I came to understand that my parents were on to something. It is this approach—combining maximum opportunity with the right incentives to succeed—that has made America great. We are a country that rewards enterprise, favors self-reliance, and fosters free enterprise. Historically, we have given Americans the incentive to take risks and achieve by viewing welfare and government entitlements as ways to help those in need, not as ways of life for the middle class. Justice requires that individual effort and reward be kept together, and we have uniquely understood that long-term dependency on government saps the spirit of entrepreneurialism that is necessary for innovation and prosperity.

But at the same time that America is an entrepreneurial nation, it is also a generous and compassionate nation. During the twentieth century, America built a safety net for those suffering hard times. Beyond private savings, we offered Americans help in securing their retirement through private pensions and the Social Security program. In the 1960s, the government created health-care programs for retirees, and those less well off.

Our social insurance strategies of the twentieth century are a critical component of our nation's social safety net— but they must be reformed if they are to exist for those in need for the twenty-first century. As currently structured, Medicare, Medicaid, and Social Security are set to implode in the face of the massive demographic shift underway. This represents both a critical moment for needed action—and an opportunity to chart a new course for renewed growth and restored promise for this century.

Too often in American politics when anyone or any party raises the issue of reform of these entitlements, the other party reverts instantly to manipulating fear. They quickly take to the airwaves with charges that the other party is out to "gut" Social Security or deny impoverished Americans medical care. But today, this tactic isn't just cynical, it's dangerous and self-defeating. Because the fact is, our major entitlement programs have expanded beyond the government's ability to sustain them in the future. If nothing changes, they will go bankrupt. This isn't a theory, it's a fact acknowledged by all nonpartisan scorekeepers and understood by an American people far ahead of Washington's political class. So those who demagogue Americans— who understand the need to address this problem—are actively complicit in the destruction of these programs. By attacking reformers, they are depriving the next generation of American retirees the promised services for which they worked and to which they contributed all their lives.

Can America be both compassionate and prosperous? Absolutely. But compassion is not a function of the welfare state, as Progressivists would have you believe. Compassion is a relationship among individuals who know and love one another as persons. Consider, for example, the difference between the way a family provides health care for its elderly members compared with the impersonal, rationed health care that government bureaucrats may, or may not, apportion depending on budgetary calculation rather than individual need. Acts of compassion can only increase by raising the level of society's general prosperity, and this comes, not by expanding the welfare state but by lowering tax, regulatory, and other government barriers to entrepreneurialism, economic growth, and new jobs.

On the other hand, the policies of President Obama and the Democratic congressional majority will do little to overcome America's economic stagnation. They will create a level of spending, deficits, and debt that's unprecedented in America. According to the CBO, the president's policies will increase spending by an amazing $5.7 trillion by 2020, equal to nearly a full quarter of the nation's economic resources. That's one quarter of the nation's economy in the hands of government. Under Washington's current policies, deficits never fall below $670 billion in the next ten years and will exceed $1 trillion by the end of the decade.

And, of course, all these deficits add up to mountains of debt. Thanks to this administration's spending, our debt as a percentage of our economy is projected to exceed 60 percent in 2010, the highest in over a half a century. By the end of the next decade, debt will consume 90 percent—90 percent!—of our GDP. The irony is that, while those advocating an expanded entitlement state would like to make America more like Europe, the levels of debt created by their policies are too high for us to join the European Union.

America is on a dangerous downward path, but it's not too late to get back on the upward road to security and solid growth. We have a handful of years to save our children and grandchildren from a life of economic decline and insecurity. If we begin to restructure our nation's entitlement programs now, we may revive, rededicate, and save the American idea.

The Wisconsinites I have been honored to represent for the last twelve years are like Americans everywhere. They can look squarely at the choices facing them and take the right path. But to make an informed choice, Americans need a sound vision of a future to which they can aspire. Republicans must rededicate ourselves to the principles that founded this nation—liberty, free enterprise, and government by the consent of the governed. Let's reapply these principles as timeless guides to meet the challenges we face and save this exceptional and blessed country in which Providence has placed the American people to live.

CHAPTER SIX

A Roadmap for America's Future

———— ★ ————

I'm a fifth-generation Wisconsin native—born and raised in Janesville, Wisconsin. I lost my dad in my formative teenage years. It forced me to grow up fast, and I've been beyond blessed to have been surrounded and supported by family and friends. I recall my dad often telling me, "Son, you're either part of the problem or part of the solution." Strangely, he usually made this point when I found myself to be part of the problem.

My dad also introduced me to our nation's historic legacy: that every generation of Americans tackles its defining challenges and leaves the next generation more prosperous, more secure, and more free. Whether the scourge of slavery and civil war, the Great Depression and the world at war, or stagflation and malaise—our parents, grandparents, and great-grandparents met our nation's challenges with purpose and courage and left the next generation with a stronger America. This is our unique legacy as Americans.

Today we face the very real threat of severing this legacy. Right now, too many in Washington are a part of the problem, not a part of the solution. Our continued acceleration down the path to bankruptcy, with a crushing burden of debt set to crash our economy, will leave the next generation with an inferior standard of living and an inability to make the most of their lives.

My father's lessons were kept in the front of my mind when I first came to Washington in my early twenties. Like I said, I had been a think tank guy, writing speeches and policy papers for Jack Kemp and Bill Bennett. But as proud as I was of the work I did for them, I knew I was on the sidelines. Strengthened by the encouragement of my family, I ran for the House seat in Wisconsin's 1st congressional district, a district that had voted for Michael Dukakis and Bill Clinton and would go on to vote for Al Gore and Barack Obama. Still, I didn't hide my limited government, free-market principles. I campaigned on them. I spoke to the voters of the 1st District like adults. And the result should be a revelation to the consultants and various other poll-driven political professionals who believe Americans have to be treated like children: I won. The Wisconsinites I serve—and Americans everywhere—deserve to be spoken to like adults. They deserve leaders who are honest about our problems and offer bold solutions to address them. Agree or disagree with me, but my electoral success in

Southern Wisconsin is the result of tireless hard work and forthright honesty. I've been straight with my employers— the residents of Wisconsin's 1st District—both before and after they gave me the opportunity and honor to serve them.

Since first elected as a twenty-eight-year-old in 1998, I have admittedly lost some of my youthfulness, but I believe that, if anything, my idealism has grown and matured. I believe in the fundamental decency and wisdom of the American people and their ability to govern themselves under a Constitution, now well over two hundred years old, that limits political power. I believe we have a right to enjoy a government that respects the American people as the true sovereign of the country, and, as the Declaration of Independence proclaims, that secures our natural God-given rights to live, be free, and fulfill all of our human potential.

I have learned a thing or two about the ways of Washington since I came here, though. One of the first lessons I learned was, even if you come to Congress believing in limited government and fiscal prudence, once you get here you are bombarded with pressure to violate your conscience and your commitment to help secure the people's natural right to equal opportunity.

Members of Congress average twenty meetings a day, in fifteen-minute increments, almost exclusively with individuals or groups who want something. Constituents have requests for more government spending on often legitimate—even commendable—projects. Interest groups want their piece of the expanding government pie. Businesses want regulations to make life easier for themselves and more difficult for their competitors. The pressure is relentless to create bigger, more expensive, and more intrusive government. Believe it or not, the people who believe in freedom and equal opportunity don't usually come by to say, "Hey, Paul! You're doing a great job! We love your views! Continue to leave us alone!" In fact it might help a lot if they did carry just that message to those who are supposed to represent us in Congress!

It was this relentless pressure to bring home the bacon that was the undoing of the Republican majority that came into office in 1994. They allowed their limited government principles to be overtaken by the pressure to appease voters and donors. As Eric has written, the Republican majority succumbed to the earmark culture. They did what the pollsters told them they needed to do to get reelected. They gathered the wish lists of the different groups in their electoral base and dispensed the goodies they requested. As long as the members brought home the bacon, they maintained their popularity and continued to get reelected.

They continued to get reelected, that is, until the corruption of the process caught up with them; until the people got wind of the Bridge to Nowhere and rightly asked why they were being asked to pay for such things; and until their colleagues and associates started going to jail.

In contrast to Republicans when they stick to their principles, the Democratic leadership is proud to head up the party of government. Think, for example, of the chairman of the House Financial Services Committee, Massachusetts democrat Barney Frank, openly proclaiming in a TV interview that his party is "trying on every front to increase the role of government." Resisting Washington's pressure to expand the state and state spending isn't an issue for these leaders. But for Republicans, staying loyal to the American principle of limited government means resisting the centrifugal forces of Washington. And our party can only do that when we have a deeper understanding of what those principles are and a publicly articulated set of solutions guided by them. If Republicans aren't anchored to their principles, it's only a matter of time in Washington before we imitate these Democratic leaders: expanding government and government spending in order to cling to power.

I admit that in recent years Republicans abandoned these principles. We lost the true path and suffered electoral defeats. But we have not returned from this experience empty handed. We have learned that unless we Republicans guide our policy decisions by the founding principles of freedom and equal opportunity, and the free-market democracy that is their practical meaning, change in America will no longer be guided by the enduring ideas that make this a great and exceptional nation. Unless Republicans promote economic and social policies rooted in the self-evident truths of equality and liberty, we will under the Progressivist ideology of today's Democratic leaders slowly fall into the mediocrity that the once great nations of Europe have become under social welfare paternalism. The real choices before us have come into view.

———— ★ ————

If there is one word that is responsible for the current majority in Washington it is "change." President Obama and the congressional Democrats rode to victory in 2008 by promising to change Washington, to change our political culture, even (although not many seemed to notice) to change America itself.

But "change" is, of course, a morally neutral word. It describes a movement . . . but in what direction? "Change" can be for the better or for the worse. As a candidate, Barack Obama cultivated the image of a centrist. He promised to rise above "ideology." But as president, Obama has proven himself to be zealously ideological. With his Progressivist allies in the Democratic leadership of Congress, he has set about fulfilling a very old vision for America, one that is meant to surrender the timeless truths on which our country was founded, and in which the vast majority of Americans have always remained loyal.

A few years back, most left-of-center pundits and politicians stopped calling themselves "liberals" and began calling themselves "Progressives." I can't say precisely why they made this switch. Perhaps they felt that something about the word "liberal" no longer sat well with the American people. But whatever the reason for the change, liberals didn't just dream up the term "Progressive." Progressivism is actually an old political movement in America, going back before the beginning of the twentieth century.

Progressivism marked the point at which some politicians and intellectuals began for the first time to question the meaning of the Constitution and the self-evident truths of the American founding. Politicians like President Woodrow Wilson, one-time professor of politics at Princeton University, argued that the Constitution should be a "living" document whose meaning had to "keep up with the times." In practice this meant whatever a Progressivist president, Congress, or Supreme Court said it was—for now. And once the Constitution's very words were no longer considered binding over time, the concept of limited government outlined in the Constitution—of government that protects our God-given rights to life, liberty, and the pursuit of happiness—was out the window. Suddenly government could create "rights"—and just as easily as it could create them, it could take them away. The central notion of the Declaration of Independence—that the people grant power to the government, the government doesn't grant power to the people—was turned upside down.

As the twentieth century unfolded, Progressivism became responsible for the increasing centralization of power in Washington. We can see its effect in the growing legions of federal bureaucrats. The Progressive doctrine holds that "experts" are professionally trained to tell average Americans how to live. So we have armies of elites running our schools, regulating our businesses, and dictating what kind of lightbulbs we should use. Progressivists don't trust the people to spend their own money well. They believe in taking more and more of the peoples' income through taxes and leaving it to government to decide how it is best spent.

The endgame of the Progressivist vision is to take America past the tipping point I talked about earlier; to create an America where dependence on government has replaced individual initiative, innovation, and imagination. The Progressivist vision is to create a new American person who no longer strives to better oneself but accepts one's station in life—and looks to government to help cope not only with difficulties but with every important personal decision. And from the enactment of the failed $1 trillion "stimulus" bill last year, to the pass-at-any cost government takeover of health care, President Obama and the Democratic leadership have zealously followed this Progressivist strategy, taking us closer to the tipping point, closer to a European-style welfare state where high taxes, big government, and double-digit unemployment become a way of life. The passivity this way of living encourages means that most people abandon the right to govern themselves, leaving bureaucratic experts and political leaders in control of every important aspect of individual and social life. A long time ago, the insightful French visitor to America, Alexis de Tocqueville, had already identified this subtle threat to America's democratic freedom as a soft kind of despotism.

The rhetoric of "change" in the 2008 election and beyond appeals both to our constant desire to improve our lives and those of the next generation, and to a deep disaffection among the American electorate. We are right to be unsatisfied with our institutions—our financial institutions, our economy, our schools, and, most of all, our government. Our hope for change that brings more freedom and prosperity is real, but abused by those that claimed to be for "change." Almost two years into the Obama presidency, it has become abundantly clear that the Democrats' Progressive vision is not the change most Americans voted for.

For Eric, Kevin, and me, the result is that it's an exciting time to be an advocate of liberty. We have a tremendous opportunity to present a different vision of change, one guided not by the soft despotism of European-style social welfarism, but by the timeless truths on which our nation was founded. We have a deep attachment and enduring faith in the Constitution and the principles of freedom that were given to us by our Founders. We feel them in our bones precisely because they are natural to all human beings. Whether you're a Democrat, a Republican, or an independent—you feel it and you know it.

Guided by our founding principles, we have the opportunity to direct "change" toward the ends that have made America the envy of the world. We're fully aware of our nation's challenges, but we reject the notion that America needs to be remade. The miracle of America is that, through our openness and entrepreneurialism, our nation is always new; we remake ourselves every day. The great achievement of our founding was to take the unchanging truths of liberty and equality and use them to build a nation that never stops changing.

No, America does not need to be remade, we just need to recommit to the ideas that have made us great. We need to rededicate ourselves to the most liberating and most inclusive idea ever conceived by man: that all human beings are created equal, with equal rights to live, to be free, to acquire property, and do all we can to fulfill our God-given potential. And we need to reconnect to the fundamental fact that the great purpose of government is to secure these rights. Protecting every person's life, liberty, and freedom to pursue happiness is the great and only mission of a government true to our founding. When government grows beyond this mission—even if the motivation is noble—it weakens freedom, reduces prosperity, and becomes arrogant and intrusive. Such a government isn't "progressive." It goes backward, finding excuses to entitle some groups at the expense of others. It suffocates individual initiative and encourages victimhood. It creates an aversion to risk that saps the entrepreneurial spirit necessary for growth, innovation, and prosperity. It replaces, in the words of the Declaration, the "laws of Nature and Nature's God" with a regulatory state of "experts" who believe government is answerable to no higher authority. It abandons constitutional limits and expands its powers into every aspect of society, centralizing control in federal bureaucracies that are not accountable to the people.

This is the point we are rapidly approaching today. And both Republicans and Democrats are responsible for bringing us here.

The president's lack of focus on our spending addiction was understandable, if regrettable, in 2002. But it is unforgivable in 2010. America stands at the brink. Our government is headed toward bankruptcy while our people are out of work. And for the last eighteen months it has been the Democrats' turn to drive us further toward the tipping point. They have done so in disregard—actually, in *direct opposition*—to the will of the American people. They have done so arrogantly and undemocratically. And they have done so in defiance of their promises made to the American people. Runaway spending, piling new unfunded entitlements on top of old unfunded entitlements, cutting backroom deals, and executing undemocratic legislative maneuvers—this is emphatically *not* the change America has been waiting for.

We deserve better from Washington. It's time that we demand more than "change." It's time that we demand a new commitment—in the form of workable solutions—to the principles that have made us great.

———— ★ ————

What would an agenda of solutions based on American principles look like?

I have put forward my specific solution, called "A Roadmap for America's Future," to meet this challenge. The Congressional Budget Office confirms that this plan achieves the goal of paying off government debt in the long run while securing the social safety net and starting up future economic growth.

The problem, in a nutshell is this: Medicare, Medicaid, and Social Security, three giant entitlements, are out of control. Exploding costs will drive our federal government and national economy to collapse. And the recession plus this Congress' spending spree have accelerated the day of reckoning.

Both Republicans and Democrats have failed to be candid about this. And we have only postponed the crisis by shaking a tin cup at China and Japan. There's a better way to save America's financial future while keeping our promises to the elderly and the needy.

A new Congress could start by making you the owner of your health plan. Under my Roadmap reform, a tax break that now benefits only those with job-based health insurance will be replaced by tax credits that benefit every American. And it secures universal access to quality, affordable health coverage with incentives that hold down health-care cost increases.

Everyone fifty-five and over will remain in the current Medicare program. For those now under fifty-five, Medicare will be like the health-care program we in Congress enjoy. Future seniors will receive a payment and pick an insurance plan from a diverse list of Medicare-certified plans—with more support for those with low incomes and higher health costs. To reform Medicaid, low-income people will receive the means to buy private health insurance like everyone else.

Under the Roadmap's Social Security proposal, everyone fifty-five and older will remain in the existing program with no change. Those under fifty-five will choose either to stay with traditional Social Security, or to join a retirement system like Congress's own plan. They will be able to invest more than a third of their payroll taxes in their own savings account, guaranteed and managed by Social Security. For both Social Security and Medicare, eligibility ages will gradually increase, and the wealthy will receive smaller benefit increases.

The Roadmap also offers a better way to get this economy moving again. It offers taxpayers an option: either use the tax code we have today, or use a simple, low-rate, two-tier personal income tax that gets rid of loopholes and the double taxation of savings and investment. It also replaces corporate income taxes with a simple, competitive 8.5 percent business consumption tax. These low-rate and simple tax reforms would provide the certainty and the incentives for investors to open new enterprises and for workers to find a marketplace expanding in new jobs.

The Roadmap plan shifts power to individuals at the

expense of government control. It rejects cradle-to-grave welfare state ideas because they drain individuals of their self-reliance. And it still honors our historic commitment to strengthening the social safety net for those who need it most.

I would welcome honest debate in the next Congress on how to tackle our fiscal crisis, as well as the larger debate on the proper role of government. It's time politicians in Washington stopped patronizing the American people as if they were children. It's time we stop deferring tough decisions and promising fiscal fantasies. It's time we tell Americans the truth, offer them a choice, and count on them to do what's right.

PART THREE

———— ★ ————

CONGRESSMAN

KEVIN McCARTHY

CHAPTER SEVEN

The Politics of Re-Earning Trust

———————— ★ ————————

Washington is full of inspiring monuments, beautiful views, and interesting historical markers. Everyone has their favorite and, as a native Californian who spends time each week in Washington, I'm no exception. But my favorite spot in the capital is a little less obvious than those typically featured on postcards or captured by photographers. When I bring visitors to Washington I like to take them to the stairs on the east side of the Capitol Building that lead up to the House Chamber.

When I walk these marble stairs—visibly worn down by countless footsteps over the years—I can't help but think of all the people who have climbed them before me. It may sound corny, but I am reminded of the responsibility I have to the people I represent.

I don't care which party you come from, if you have ever

walked these stairs, you walk into the United States Capitol as an American.

Candidates frequently ask me how long they should serve. My response is always, "When you walk into this building and you don't get goose bumps, you should leave."

———————— ★ ————————

Just like Eric and Paul, politics for me has always been about fighting for something bigger than myself; about making a difference, not just serving time. When I came to Washington in January 2007, my freshman Republican colleagues and I were the only House Republicans to have never served during the twelve-year House Republican majority. But we had watched and learned from how they lost their majority. I was determined not to become a part of the entrenched incumbent mindset but to change it. I still feel that way, which is why I am working so hard to help as many like-minded candidates as I can serve in Congress.

Some people come to their political beliefs through the beliefs of their parents. But for me, there was nothing automatic about becoming a Republican. Growing up in Bakersfield, my family were Democrats. My dad was a fire-fighter and moved furniture on his days off. Still, like lots of Americans we used to be called "Reagan Democrats," and from an early age I believed that fiscal conservatism and limited government were the keys to growth and opportunity for all Americans. I have always felt it was important for people to put their talents to work for the ideas and causes they believe in. Work hard and do the best you can at the job in front of you, and the rewards will follow.

I also learned early that you have to have the good sense to recognize opportunity when it comes knocking. I had been working as a seasonal firefighter, using some of the money I earned to buy used cars in Los Angeles, fix them up, and sell them for a modest profit in Bakersfield. Soon after I graduated from high school, the second day after the California State Lottery started offering scratch-off tickets, I casually bought one, thinking nothing would come of it. So no one was more surprised than I was when I won. The payout was small by today's standards, just $5,000. But it was enough to get me started as a small businessman.

I invested my lottery winnings in the stock market and when I was nineteen, I opened my first real business, a deli in Bakersfield. Running my sandwich shop taught me what all small businesspeople learn: that the work is hard, the margins are thin, and the government is too often an obstacle, not an aid, to success. Still, I tried to be innovative and stay ahead of the competition. For instance, we offered a superior sandwich by ordering and using freshly baked bread every day—a practice that would later be trumpeted by a familiar nationwide sandwich company.

With a lot of hard work and dedication I built my sandwich shop into a successful business and sold it to pay for my college education, including a master's in business administration from California State University, Bakersfield. Translating my business success into a higher education, I think, made me more sensitive to other small-business owners who are relying on their success to send themselves and their kids to school. This lesson has stayed with me. Helping the small businesses and entrepreneurs who create jobs in our communities has always been a central focus of my work whether in Sacramento or in Washington.

Then, at the ripe old age of twenty-two, I noticed an ad in the local paper saying that my congressman, Bill Thomas, was looking for students interested in his paid summer internship program in DC. Congressman Thomas was someone whose career in Congress I had long followed and admired. So I immediately applied—and was rejected. Those who know me will not be surprised to learn that I did not take this rejection as final. I went back to Representative Thomas's office and said, "Okay, if you won't pay me to work for you, is there anything I can do for you for free?" My tenacity—not to mention my price—must have won over the congressman because he put me to work in the district office cutting clips from the local newspapers and doing office scut work.

My first experience in public service was a modest one, but it was a turning point for me. It was an opportunity to learn about the legislative and political process, as well as the issues and concerns that mattered to voters in the district. I ended up spending fifteen years working for Representative Thomas, ending my time as district director.

Looking back, I now know that my unpaid internship with Representative Thomas literally set the course for my future in public service. It's a shame that President Obama earlier in 2010 pandered to his union boss supporters and targeted unpaid internships for elimination. Now that I'm in Congress I offer as many summer internships in my office as space will allow. I know firsthand the opportunity that can grow out of getting a chance to work and learn. Especially in Washington, a summer internship can lead to a career serving a cause you believe in.

Helping Representative Thomas represent the 22nd District was much more than a job for me. It was—and is—that motivation I mentioned earlier; the cause greater than myself for which I have devoted my career.

★

As a fourth-generation Kern County resident I have deep roots in the district. My great-grandfather, Jeremiah McCarthy, became a Kern County cattle rancher in 1883. I have lived in Bakersfield my whole life and continue to return home from Washington every week.

It was this passion for our county, the Central California region, and state that led me to run for the California

State Assembly in 2002. I was proud to represent my home county in Sacramento. And I was proud to be unanimously selected as the Republican leader of the State Assembly (the first freshman ever to be so selected).

My work in the Assembly focused on the major issues facing the state: the budget, workers compensation, taxes, and economic competitiveness. Serving in the minority, I learned the importance of engaging and working across the aisle whenever possible while still fighting for the principles I believe in.

As Republican leader, I also began a process that would serve me well as a candidate, as a party leader, and which I continue to use today. I traveled the state learning about my colleagues, their districts, and their concerns. I have found that when you travel to someone's district, you understand them better; understand their issues and why they fight for what they fight for. There is no substitute for getting to know the people and issues firsthand.

When my mentor and friend Bill Thomas decided to retire in 2006, I felt strongly this was an opportunity to further serve my neighbors and my state—this time in Washington. I quickly went to work building the support I knew would be needed. I was fortunate to be able to attract significant support and went on to win the Republican primary.

Just as I had as Republican leader in the California Assembly, as a candidate for the U.S. House of Representatives I set out to travel the country visiting other Republican candidates and learning about the issues affecting their districts. They would, I hoped, be my future colleagues. I wanted to start building relationships and help bring more allies to Congress for the hard work that I knew lay ahead.

But it was while traveling the country in 2006 that I came to the shocking realization that my party was going to lose its majority in the House. I knew going in that it was going to be a tough election for Republicans, but I didn't grasp just how bad it would be until I began visiting districts across the country. There was a deep disconnect between what Republican leaders in Washington were saying and what I, as a first-time congressional candidate, was hearing in my district and on the ground elsewhere.

Ironically, back then it was the Republican Party that was accusing the Democrats of being the "Party of No." Democrats were attempting to nationalize the election and focus on the complacency and corruption of Republicans. Republicans were firing back that Democrats were only interested in obstructing their majority. The Republican Party leadership back in Washington was convinced that the old truism about how "all politics is local" would save them from the Democrats' attempt to nationalize the election. They clung to the belief that there was no broad discontent in the country. They had introduced the right bills and had the right talking points. Things might be tough, they thought, but the voters were still with them.

But as I traveled around the country, I began to know better. I was on the ground meeting with the candidates;

walking their districts, eating with them at the local Bob Evans and sitting in on their town halls. Voters were deeply unhappy with Republicans. They weren't focused on the issues the leadership assumed the election would be about. They were talking about the party's failures—our failures—from high-profile ethical lapses to the inability to rein in spending or even slow the growth of government.

The Republican base was angry about the way the party had betrayed its principles with earmarks that lacked the transparency and accountability that the public expected when taxpayer dollars were spent. At the same time, the party had lost the trust of many independents. The result was that no one was motivated to go out and do the work necessary for congressional Republicans to win. Incumbents in safe seats were fighting for their lives. The party brand was so damaged that Republican candidates didn't want the party leadership in Washington coming to their districts to campaign. And yet that same leadership still believed that the majority was safe.

They were wrong. Democrats gained thirty-one seats and a majority in the House, ending twelve years of Republican control.

But even in that disastrous year, we had some successes. The thirteen Republican freshmen who were elected to the House of Representatives in 2006 constituted the smallest freshman class since 1914. But despite its small size, our class included many bright and talented people whom I still serve with today—Doug Lamborn of Colorado, Gus

Bilirakis and Vern Buchanan of Florida, Peter Roskam of Illinois, Michele Bachmann of Minnesota, Adrian Smith of Nebraska, Dean Heller of Nevada, Jim Jordan of Ohio, Mary Fallin of Oklahoma (and then later, through special elections, Paul Broun of Georgia, Bob Latta of Ohio, Rob Wittman of Virginia, and Steve Scalise of Louisiana). These are the men and women who are in many ways the future of the party.

Despite my experience and background, I obviously had a lot to learn as a freshman legislator in Congress. And I was determined to do the work necessary to represent my district and live up to the ideals and promises I had made during the campaign.

I was also determined not to be satisfied with being in the minority. I thought about something former House Republican leader Bob Michel, the Republican from Illinois, used to say to newly elected GOP members during the Democrats' forty-year majority reign prior to 1994. Michel was quoted as saying, "Every day I wake up and look in the mirror and say to myself, 'Today you're going to be a loser.' And after you're here awhile, you'll start to feel the same way. But don't let it bother you. You'll get used to it."

I wasn't about to get used to being in the minority. To accomplish what I wanted to accomplish—rein in spending and put Washington back on the side of the people—we needed a majority that shared these beliefs. Building on what I had learned in the 2006 campaign, I knew it was time to go on the offensive.

———— ★ ————

In 2007, Republicans were in the minority by twenty seats in the House. We were badly outnumbered and our party brand was in shambles. We had lost our reputation both as the party of responsible spending and as the party that keeps America safe. But from my experience in the 2006 election, I knew there were candidates out there who could help us not only change our image but change the direction of the country. I had known Eric and Paul back from when I was a candidate for the 22nd District. I knew they shared my desire to change the direction of the country as well as my eagerness to find the reinforcements we needed. So we got together and began to talk about what we could do. I could tell right away that we were thinking in the same terms about how to begin to rebuild. We had to begin working from the ground up.

The first step was admitting how the party had lost its way. Under Republican leadership in the early 2000s, spending and government got out of control. And as government grew, there were scandals and political compromises. The focus became getting reelected rather than solving problems and addressing pressing issues.

We knew that if we were to start the rebuilding process that would lead to the party's rebirth we needed to focus on both policy and political strategy. We knew that if we were going to earn back the voters' trust we would have to do more than just oppose the policies of the Democratic majority. We had to offer creative and effective solutions of our own. We had to get better at not only crafting solutions to the real problems the country faced but communicating those ideas to voters and proving that we could live up to our ideals.

We had to offer the right policy solutions, and we had to practice smart politics. For me, politics is about people and ideas. Politics is how our democracy works in practice. It's individual Americans with competing ideas and competing visions. That's why, along with all the policy briefs, memos, and reports that I take on my weekly flights from California to Washington, I also include the *Almanac of American Politics*, the political junkie's bible. I enjoy learning about districts all over America and thinking about how we can communicate our ideas more effectively to the voters there.

One of the advantages of being the minority party to the current Democratic majority in Washington was that, since we had so little opportunity to shape legislation, we had time to take stock of what Congress was doing and how well we were serving the American people. Every three months or so, whenever we could find the time—sometimes late in the evening—I got my Republican freshman colleagues together and we shared an hour on the House floor to talk about our quarterly "report card" of Congress. We didn't have any illusions that the whole nation was watching us, but since the new House Democratic majority had effectively shut us out of the legislative process, we decided to devote this hour of time to hold the majority's feet to the fire.

Accountability ought to be a bipartisan exercise. And the Democratic majority's partisan legislation gave us plenty of ammunition to talk about the lack of accountability in Congress. This included how they junked up war-spending bills with earmarks for things like peanut storage facilities. It included letting the American people know that current members of Congress actually had the audacity to ask for taxpayer money to fund centers named after themselves—their own personal "Monuments to Me" (in one case, it was an earmark, exposed by my good friend Rep. John Campbell from California, that Rep. Charlie Rangel (D-NY) requested for a City College of New York library and conference room—named after him, of course). And it included showing how much House Democrats continued to increase deficit spending, hurting our economy and competitiveness.

The more we did these report cards, and the more I looked at the failing state of our economy, the more I was reminded of a book I frequently recommend: *Good to Great* by Jim Collins. When I read the different stories in this book, my mind always settles at the same question: Why do some leaders settle for mediocrity, while others continue to push the envelope? When I look at an unemployment rate that has meant hardship to millions of American families and a failed "stimulus" that did not create the jobs promised, and then I listen to the president and the Democratic

House leadership blame others by talking about how they inherited this economy, I see American leaders settling for mediocrity. At what point did we decide to tolerate joblessness, to tolerate mediocre results when government spends hundreds of billions of dollars it doesn't have? We need to constantly look in the mirror and ask ourselves whether we, as representatives and public servants, have met the expectations of the American people, and then whether we could have done more.

In any case, these "report card" sessions also gave us the opportunity to discuss our conservative principles, and how they could be applied to a set of solutions to combat the Democrats' high-spending earmark culture. Since we had never been part of the previous Republican majority, we knew better than most how badly our party needed to remake itself as the party of reform again. Republicans had been part of the problem and we were determined to remake our party as part of the solution.

Adding urgency to our effort was the beginning of the country's descent into economic crisis in 2007. Although the economy was still growing for most of the year, home values were plummeting, robbing Americans of the value of their greatest asset. More and more families fell behind on their mortgages and began to default. And the falling housing values began to have an effect on the credit markets. Something bad was heading our way.

CHAPTER EIGHT

Young Guns

———— ★ ————

As I traveled around the country in 2007, some Republican candidates were saying to me that the party had
lost so much trust with the people that they didn't want
the party leadership coming to their districts to campaign
for them. They were interested, however, in having rising
Republican leaders like Eric Cantor and Paul Ryan come
to their districts. This new generation of pro-market, small
government leaders filled such a need that in October Fred
Barnes of *The Weekly Standard* profiled us and christened
us the "young guns."

One evening that same month, I was meeting with my
good friend John Gard, former Wisconsin assembly speaker
and one of the best candidates I had met in 2006. We were
talking about him running again and he mentioned he had
seen the article. It would be helpful, he said, if one of us

could visit his district and campaign for him. That got me thinking, and I approached Eric and Paul about the idea of traveling together, as "Young Guns," to visit Republican candidates interested in a new approach for the party. That way, their neighbors and communities could see that we were all working hard to reconnect our party with the American people.

As weeks and months went by, what began as an informal way to support like-minded candidates became a more formal structure. Once we had studied the candidate and given him or her our support to become a Young Gun, we wanted to make sure we provided a long-term relationship with that candidate. That meant we committed to providing financial support through our campaign committees, visiting the candidates in their districts, but also offering mentoring sessions on what the Democrats were doing in Washington. In order to protect vulnerable Democratic members from tough votes, the House Democratic leadership would often attempt to shield their votes with procedural tricks. We realized that our candidates often wondered what these House procedures meant, so we gave them the inside scoop.

We also knew that we weren't the only current House Republicans eager to change our party, change Washington, and change the course of America. So we began approaching our colleagues with a simple pitch: are we willing to help ourselves by being proactive and going on offense to change this House? I took the fact that dozens and dozens of our House Republican colleagues joined our Young Guns effort as one of many signs that our party had shifted. Members of Congress balance a lot of different responsibilities that eat up their schedules and energy, so when so many agreed to undertake this effort voluntarily to help mentor and financially support the next generation of would-be House Republican members, I knew that Eric, Paul, and I had found a reservoir of untapped energy. The growing frustration that the country was moving in the wrong direction had created a solidarity of purpose among House Republicans to work harder to promote and protect our vision of what America could be.

★

Still, by the time it was over, the 2008 election proved that the voters were not done punishing the Republican Party. On Election Day, the Democrats increased their majority in the House by twenty-one seats. In the Senate, they had gained eight seats. To top it off, Barack Obama became president to give his party firm and unified control of Washington.

Nonetheless, in that hostile political environment, the growing Young Guns organization had some significant successes. With the economy now officially in recession and Washington busy bailing out corporations while Americans lost their jobs and their homes, our message was beginning to take hold. We weren't just another political money machine, picking the candidates with the deepest pockets and the best name identification. We supported candidates who were focused on fiscal responsibility, limited government and accountability. We were also interested in *not* repeating the mistakes of the previous Republican majority. We concentrated on bringing new perspectives and fresh ideas to Washington.

In the end, of the five Democratic incumbents that lost their seats in 2008, four of them were beaten by Young Guns challengers, and three Young Guns candidates also won races in open seats. This obviously wasn't enough to reverse the fortunes of the GOP, but each victory was important and gave us something to build on.

More importantly, these victories weren't just notches on our party's belt. Each of our successful candidates were solid, limited-government, pro-market conservatives.

LYNN JENKINS

Everything that was difficult about the 2008 election was reflected in the 2008 race for the 2nd congressional district of Kansas. Five-term Republican representative Jim Ryun had lost in 2006 to Republican-turned-Democrat Nancy

Boyda. Ryun was running again but facing primary opposition from State Treasurer Lynn Jenkins. Jenkins ended up narrowly winning the difficult primary.

It was important that the party put the primary behind us and focus on taking back this district. Nancy Boyda called herself a moderate Democrat, but in Washington she supported the liberal Democratic majority and their policy agenda. In the general election she tried to hide from her own party knowing that it did not fit well with the Republican nature of her district. She even went so far as to skip the Democratic National Convention in Denver.

In contrast, Jenkins was a great fit for our program: a proven leader with the experience and track record voters could trust. Jenkins, a certified public accountant for over twenty years, was elected State Treasurer of Kansas in 2002 and reelected four years later. Prior to her service as state treasurer she had served four years in the Kansas State Legislature.

Lynn was clearly a talented and experienced statewide candidate who understood Kansas voters. And her background as a CPA and experience as state treasurer matched up well with the growing concerns about the economy and the lack of fiscal discipline in Washington.

Lynn campaigned on making tax cuts permanent, cutting spending to reduce the deficit, and providing additional smart tax relief to the struggling middle class. Kansans respected her experience and commitment to fiscal responsibility, limited government, and political account-ability. She went on to defeat Nancy Boyda 51%–46%, regaining a seat we had lost just two years before.

ERIK PAULSEN

In the 3rd District of Minnesota we faced a different prob-lem in the retirement of Republican Rep. Jim Ramstad. Ramstad was serving his ninth term in Congress when he announced he would not run again in 2008. As soon as the announcement was made, the seat was designated by many prognosticators as a potential Democratic pickup. We knew we had to find a way to stem the tide and hold our own in open seats like this one if we were going to change the momentum.

The Democrats had what they thought was the perfect candidate to win the seat given the so-called "Blue Wave" that was believed to be sweeping the country. Ashwin Madia was an attorney and Iraq War veteran whose parents had moved to Plymouth, Minnesota, from Mumbai, India. Madia had beaten the Democratic establishment candi-dates in the primary thanks to strong liberal support and his antiwar views. He was a first time candidate but seemed well suited to the political environment and raised over $2 million.

Madia was a good candidate, but we had one better in

Erik Paulsen. Erik and I had a lot of similarities, having both been a businessman and a public servant (and later, during the campaign, I also learned something else— we were born in the same Bakersfield hospital just three months apart). He had served in the state legislature and had been chosen to serve in leadership (in his case as majority leader in the Minnesota House of Representatives). He had also worked for Congressman Ramstad as legislative director and director of his home office in Minnesota. In addition to his public service experience, Erik also brought sixteen years of business experience to the campaign.

And while Erik campaigned for the ideals we all supported, what made him stand out was his hard work. Erik in many ways simply outworked his opponent to win by eight points in a very tough environment and a district that Democrats had targeted as a potential pickup.

AARON SCHOCK

Another state legislator who worked hard and found a way to win in a tough environment was Aaron Schock in the 18th congressional district of Illinois. Aaron brought a unique combination of youth and enthusiasm and yet a surprising amount of experience to the campaign.

Aaron began his political career when he was nineteen by running for the local school board in Peoria, incredibly defeating the incumbent board president as a write-in candidate. Two years later he had risen to board president himself—the youngest in its history. This would begin a pattern.

Aaron went on to become state representative at age twenty-three—again making him the youngest member of that body. In an interesting twist, Schock shared the 2007 Illinois Committee for Honest Government "Outstanding Legislative and Constituent Service" award with then-Sen. Barack Obama. After two very effective terms as a state representative he decided to run for Congress in 2008 after moderate Republican Ray LaHood announced his retirement.

Running for an open seat in Barack Obama's home state with a struggling state party and an unpopular national party was a big challenge. The open seat was even dubbed a "once-in-a-century" opportunity for the Democrats to pick up.

Schock went on to win nearly 60 percent of the vote in a three-way race. And once again he was the youngest member—this time of the United States House of Representatives.

A lot has been made of Aaron's youth but what is remarkable about his career is the way he has connected with voters at every level and gone on to achieve success. He understands the hard work involved and he brings not only the enthusiasm of youth but also the communication styles and tools of a younger generation. It is exciting to see this generational change begin to remake the Republican Party.

So while 2008 was still a very difficult year we felt like we were making progress. Our Young Guns candidates proved that Republicans could—with the right focus, commitment, and strategy—still field great candidates and win tough elections.

———— ★ ————

Another lesson Eric, Paul, and I have learned over these years in the minority is the importance of using technology and the latest communication tools to educate, communicate, and build relationships with each other, the voters, and potential supporters.

I have always been an avid reader, even more so now that I travel cross-country every week. Since I was the Republican leader in the California State Assembly I have recommended reading material to my colleagues. And one way I found to get more members reading and absorbing new ideas was through listening, to material on an iPod. One of the first things I did was to make sure every Assembly Republican had one. I wanted our members to interact with technology and culture in the same way their constituents did—and at the same time take advantage of these tools to better learn different perspectives and communicate our message.

But for Congress it has turned out—surprise!—that the

absorption of emerging technologies and communication tools happens very slowly. The technological advances that have occurred over the past two decades have provided a lot of efficiencies and accountability in the private sector, where on-time inventories and online publication of information has improved business productivity and transparency. I am a strong advocate of adapting with technology to make government more effective, more transparent, and more accountable.

One area where Congress has a lot of room to improve is legislative transparency. Why must the public and, frankly, many members of Congress and their staffs, have to wait until the day of the vote to read the text of spending bills? These bills can and should be posted on the Internet at least a week before the vote. And why must the powerful Rules Committee, which sets the ground rules for debate and amendments to bills, be one of the few committees to not regularly televise its hearings? Shining sunlight on the process promotes accountability and public trust in government.

Technology can also be used to improve direct communications between the people and their government. From my first months in Congress, I quickly adopted tele–town hall technology in order to provide an ongoing and convenient way for my constituents to share their concerns and ideas with me, and for me to listen to what their priorities were.

I also wanted to expand communication outreach beyond the normal press statements and snail mail letters, and tailor news updates to the different ways more and more people were getting their information, such as through social media networks like Facebook, YouTube, and Twitter. As it happens, mass communications between members of Congress and their constituents is controlled by something called the Franking Commission. And the Franking Commission is part of the Committee on House Administration, a committee of which I am a member. But the Franking Commission, like so much of government, is clearly not orientated toward the latest technology and was reluctant to change. It took me eighteen months of battling the bureaucracy to bring communications between members of Congress and the American people into the twenty-first century.

To me the issue was simple: if our constituents are using these tools to communicate and to receive information, why shouldn't Congress use them to stay in touch? Congress should be as open and transparent as possible, and adapt to changing times in order to engage with all Americans, and these tools were additional ways to do it.

In the same way I fought for Congress as a whole to be able to use modern communication tools, I wanted to be sure that our Republican members and leadership were using this technology effectively.

For example, Eric and I unleashed something called WhipCast, an application crafted for the iPod and the Blackberry that allows members and the public to keep more closely in touch with what is happening in Congress and on the House floor.

And it isn't just about pushing information out. A critical aspect of regaining trust with voters is listening. We have to listen to voters and prove to them that we hear their concerns and are taking action based on the principles we have committed ourselves to.

When I was appointed by Republican leader John Boehner to be chairman of the Republican Platform Committee for the 2008 National Convention along with my good friend from North Carolina and fellow cochair, Sen. Richard Burr, I made getting input a high priority. Working with the party's e-campaign director, Cyrus Krohn, we developed an interactive online platform tool so that everyone could contribute their ideas for consideration and could do so from the convenience of their homes and at their own schedules. Previously there had been occasional town halls or regional meetings but that structure ended up limiting participation.

Using the power of the Web we ended up attracting over 130,000 viewers on the site in less than two months and had thousands of submissions. The eventual platform that was created and approved unanimously was built with the ideas of America, and can be viewed at *www.gop .com/2008platform.com*. We received national media coverage for this innovative and interactive approach. The Democratic Platform Chair, then-Arizona governor Janet Napolitano, even pledged to follow our lead and open up her party's process (a promise she failed to keep).

And in the party platform, we agreed with many people that felt that energy prices, our economy, and fiscal accountability in Washington were important priorities by proposing "accelerated exploration, drilling, and development in America" through an all-of-the-above American energy plan, advocating "lower taxes, reasonable regulation and smaller, smarter government," and imposing "an immediate moratorium on the earmarking system," something I am pleased that my House Republican colleagues agreed to do in March of 2010.

The world is changing and Republicans are changing with it. Eric, Paul, and I are determined that the GOP be the party of innovation and new ideas in both policy and technology. To this end we have been experimenting with technologies that will allow us to more effectively interact with constituents and voters in our districts and on the campaign trail; from handheld PDA applications for door-to-door campaign activities and phone banks to interactive tools that allow voters to give feedback and for us to sort and prioritize their suggestions and ideas.

---- ★ ----

It is an understatement to say that we Republicans were on our heels after the 2008 election. For the first time since 1992, there was unified Democratic control of both sides of Pennsylvania Avenue and President Barack Obama won a historic election. One of the first things we knew we had to tackle was changing our defensive mindset and insisting on the best solutions for America. From a legislative front, the stimulus bill in January 2009 provided our first opportunity to go on offense. We offered the president our cooperation by providing him an alternative proposal that would create twice as many jobs at half the cost of the Democratic bill, and when the Pelosi-led Congress rejected our proposal and dared us to resist the president's first signature legislative initiative, we stood united on principle and opposed the stimulus because it was bad policy. And based on the jobs that the stimulus promised but has failed to deliver, we were right. As the months passed, we continued to see Democrats vote for bills that spent too much, taxed too much, and borrowed too much. We needed to hold them accountable for their votes—especially vulnerable Democrats who promised fiscal sanity to the conservative districts they represented.

For inspiration, I looked to one of my heroes from World War II. Lieutenant Colonel James "Jimmy" Doolittle planned and led the first strike on a Japanese home island in the aftermath of the sneak attack on Pearl Harbor. His mission became known as the Doolittle Raid. In his autobiography, Doolittle himself explained the raid's significance this way:

> The Japanese had been told they were invulnerable. An attack on the Japanese homeland would cause confusion in the minds of the Japanese people

and sow doubt about the reliability of their leaders. There was a second, equally important, psychological reason for this attack. . . . Americans badly needed a morale boost.

Obviously comparing politics to war is a bit of a stretch, but in strategic terms I knew that to build new Republican confidence, we needed a Doolittle Raid of our own. We had just experienced a stunning loss and had seen the ground shift under our feet. We had to regain our morale and begin to go on the offensive; to chip away at the Democrats' invulnerable mindset.

Sitting around with other Young Guns members, we came up with the idea of going after vulnerable Democrats in Republican-leaning districts. Quite frankly, it was time for us to stop dwelling on the past and begin working to regain the seats we had lost; earning and regaining the voters' trust.

So Young Guns, through the National Republican Congressional Committee (NRCC), rolled out the campaign. We went after Democrats with radio ads and phone calls alerting voters to the fact that their representatives talked a good game in their conservative-leaning district but when they got to Washington they marched in lock step with ultra-liberal Nancy Pelosi. We were trying to plant the seed in voters' minds that the image they had of their elected officials was different than the reality of what was happening in Washington.

Now obviously this Young Guns campaign was not a magic bullet that would automatically lead to our defeating scores of freshman Democratic legislators or to reclaiming the majority. We had, and still have, a lot of work to do. But the campaign was a great success because it changed the focus from our losses in the past to going on the offensive and working hard to regain what we had lost—to *earning* the majority.

———— ★ ————

Young Guns was helping to go on offense. But even after demonstrating that Democrats in Republican-leaning districts promised one thing in their districts, and then voted for another thing in Washington, we needed to make sure that we were also fielding good, fresh-thinking candidates to provide voters in those districts with a credible Republican alternative for the 2010 elections.

Even though 2008 was a very tough year for Republicans, there was much to learn from some of the successes of the Young Guns program. The program worked well in concert and through the support and leadership of then-NRCC chairman Tom Cole. And after the election, under the leadership of NRCC chairman Pete Sessions, the NRCC adopted our program as the key candidate recruitment and training program for House Republicans and named me to be the chief recruiter for the 2010 election.

My first goal was to help create a process that provides a system of clear and tailored benchmarks for candidates to meet so that we are helping the best possible and most committed candidates build successful campaigns. Working with Eric and Paul, and together with Chairman Sessions and his very capable NRCC staff, we created three levels of candidates, from "On the Radar" to "Contender" to "Young Gun." Candidates are named to the program by meeting individualized benchmarks set by the committee. This process is designed to ensure that candidates earn support by creating and using the necessary tools and strategies for a successful modern political campaign. Benchmarks include setting and developing fundraising goals and a fundraising system; a volunteer database and recruitment goals; an e-mail list, press lists, and communications strategies; and media training, connecting with vendors and other measures. You can see some of our candidates by visiting the Young Guns website: *www.GOPYoungGuns.com*.

My second goal was to create a team of committed House Republicans to help me with recruiting. It was quiet and anonymous work that we did at daybreak every Thursday morning throughout 2009. We would familiarize ourselves with districts and compare notes on potential candidates we talked to and who needed a phone call or a district visit. Our success has been due to the persistence and energy of our recruitment team—Tom Price and Lynn

Westmoreland of Georgia, Judy Biggert of Illinois, Geoff Davis of Kentucky, Jim Jordan of Ohio, Bill Shuster of Pennsylvania, Pete Olson of Texas, Jason Chaffetz of Utah, Rob Wittman of Virginia, and Cathy McMorris Rodgers of Washington. Our goal was to initially field enough top-tier candidates in forty districts (the number we needed to win the majority). As the political climate changed with Speaker Pelosi's overreaching on issues like cap and trade, government bailouts, and continued record deficit spending and debt, we hit our goal of forty districts ahead of schedule, and changed our target to eighty districts.

Then, in the summer of 2009, the Tea Party protests and the health-care town hall meetings happened. I remember watching many different town halls, and more than anything, it became apparent that something on the ground had changed. Americans were promised hope and change, but House Democratic leaders read that mandate with a heavier emphasis on government control, mandates, and taxes than Americans wanted.

Coincidentally, in the middle of August, I had planned to join one of the hardest workers (and genuinely down-to-earth guys) in our Republican conference, Rep. Lynn Westmoreland of Georgia, and the always-astute NRCC political director Brian Walsh on a road trip across America to visit districts and recruit candidates. We drove through Illinois, Iowa, and Wisconsin (inadvertently due to a wrong turn on the highway), and then flew to North Carolina and Tennessee. All told we met dozens of community leaders and businessmen who previously had little interest in running for Congress, but felt compelled to consider it because of the extreme agenda the Democrats in Washington were forcing through. It wasn't just the liberal policies they objected to, it was the fact that the economy was continuing to decline and the unemployment numbers were continuing to rise but the focus of Washington was on everything but job creation.

But there was one person who caught my eye when we were recruiting in Tennessee: Stephen Fincher. He walked into the room we were in and said: "Mr. Kevin, my name's Stephen Fincher, and I'm from Frog Jump, Tennessee. I'm a farmer, and I'm concerned about where this country's going."

Stephen in many ways epitomizes the type of candidates Young Guns is trying to recruit. Stephen was working hard in life—growing cotton, corn, soybeans, and wheat on his family farm, and staying involved in the community through his other family "business": the "Fincher Family" singing ministry songs at more than a hundred events annually. But like many Americans, just a few months ago, he was watching his country change in ways he never dreamed, and he told us: "How am I going to answer my children in the future when they ask me, 'What did you do when the country changed? Did you stand up and fight?' "

Stephen Fincher ended up fighting. After we met, he decided to run for Congress in Tennessee's 8th District against Rep. John Tanner, an entrenched incumbent who hadn't faced serious opposition since 1994 and had more than $1 million in his campaign fund. But through hard work and the trust of his family and friends, Stephen barnstormed the district and raised a spectacular $1 million. His momentum and the changing political environment had an impact: Tanner announced he would not seek reelection! Stephen epitomizes what Young Guns is all about—and his commitment to bringing fiscal sanity, accountability, and fresh ideas is sorely needed in Congress.

Meeting Fincher and engaging in conversations with other potential candidates and Americans from all over the country that August made clear to me that the ground was shifting. Americans wanted solutions, but not the Democratic solutions that were being offered in Washington. And truth be told, they were not looking for partisan solutions from Republicans. They wanted commonsense American solutions that addressed the priorities of the day.

Moving forward, Young Guns and all our hard work has to be about something bigger than who wins or who loses; it can't be about politicians, it has to be about solutions. Everything we do has to be filtered through the recognition that the status quo is unacceptable—that Washington business as usual is what we are fighting against.

I remember a conversation I had with a potential candidate that illustrates this point. I sat down with the candidate and his wife to discuss the possibility of his running for Congress. Our conversation went something like this:

KEVIN McCARTHY: Are you going to run?

CANDIDATE: Do you need me to run?

KM: No, I don't need you to run.

CANDIDATE: Do you want me to run?

KM: No, *I* don't want you to run. I'll help you if *you want* to run.

By the time the meeting had ended, I told him not to run: "This can't be about you. This is about changing America."

What I said may seem harsh, but it's true. We aren't looking just to fill slots. We are looking for the future leaders of the Republican Party. Of course, I want the Republican Party to do well. But more importantly, I want America to do well.

CHAPTER NINE

A Commitment to America

———— ★ ————

Two thousand and nine was a year of great contrasts for Eric, Paul, and me. On the one hand, it was the year we saw our country accelerate in a direction that, if unchanged, will destroy what is best about us.

On the other hand, 2009 was the year that those of us in Congress who believe there's a better way to lead our country came together, created commonsense solutions to our challenges, and fought together for them as one.

When Eric became Republican whip in January of 2009, I was honored to be named his chief deputy whip. Together with Paul as the head Republican on the Budget Committee, we set out to be constructive partners with the Democratic majority in addressing the nation's flagging economy. As Eric and Paul have already mentioned, there was no partisan advantage for us in obstructing progress on getting Americans back to work, despite what the Demo-crats claim. If we were seen as simply obstacles to progress, the voters would punish us even more.

So we began a process of carefully crafting alternatives to the Democrats' big spending, big government bills. On the stimulus, on cap and trade, housing and health care, we presented real alternatives; commonsense solutions at a time of record-breaking deficit spending that would fix America's problems without destroying what America is all about. But despite the victories of commonsense conser-vatives in Virginia, New Jersey, and Massachusetts—and thanks to backroom deals and antidemocratic maneuver-ing on the part of the Democrats—our alternative solutions lost. And for all the talk of Republican obstructionism, our legislative alternatives oftentimes were the only ones to attract bipartisan support. We fought the good fight, we had the good ideas, but to change the direction of the coun-try, we don't yet have the votes.

That's why strategy is important—why politics is important—because it is the vehicle we use to achieve the goals we have set for ourselves and for our country. You can't implement policies that reflect this country's ideals and values without strategic thinking and planning. You can't avoid "politics" in a participatory democracy. It is part of the process we use to debate, deliberate, and evaluate ideas, policies, and elected officials.

Democrats and Democratic ideas in Washington have failed. The current majority has stopped listening to the people. Democrats have been governing in spite of the American people, not on behalf of them. The result is that all of the indications so far this election—the polls, the caliber of candidates we've been able to recruit, the elections in Virginia, New Jersey, and Massachusetts—point toward a historic opportunity on behalf of commonsense American values in 2010. Americans are very frustrated with the arrogance they're seeing in Washington. That doesn't mean they're happy with Republicans, but they're ready for leadership that reflects their beliefs, not defies them. The election this year is about much more than health care, or energy policy, or even the security of our country. Will we repeal TARP and unwind the vast amounts of government spending and mandates that distorts the innovation and free enterprise in our financial services industry, our health-care system, our car companies, and our energy sector? Will we take meaningful steps to cut hundreds of billions of dollars in federal spending, so we can ratchet back the deficit spending and the ballooning $12 trillion national debt that we owe to creditors like China and the Middle East? What Democrats in Washington don't understand is that when we vote no to their policies, it's not because we are trying to obstruct. It's because we are trying to protect what has worked through the history of our nation. It's about America. It's about the direction we're headed. For over a year and a half—since we stood fast together around an alternative stimulus bill that would create twice the jobs at half the cost—Republicans led by a new generation of leadership have been earning back the majority in Congress. And as of this spring, we have set forth an unprecedented engagement with the American people.

There really is nothing more powerful and inspirational than the common voice of the common man. Over the last year, we've heard those voices in town halls in every corner of this country. But under the current leadership in Washington, the voices and opinions of Americans all over the country have been ignored.

Republicans are putting an end to that. By launching America Speaking Out, we are lifting the Democratic gag rule that has been in place and instead using all the tools available—from the Internet to town hall meetings to phone apps—to empower Americans with opportunities to bring forward their concerns about America's direction, and voice their solutions to help shape America's future. Central to this project is the new innovative and interactive online forum that you can find at *www.AmericaSpeakingOut.com.*

The America Speaking Out project (which Republican Leader John Boehner appointed me to chair and which my good friend Rep. Peter Roskam from Illinois will be vice-chairing) will lead to a governing agenda that is a product of the American people. On jobs, national defense, and government transparency, this will replace the empty political rhetoric of the current majority. This is the voice of the people made concrete and quantifiable, and this will be the benchmark by which Americans can judge the actions of

House Republicans—we will stand for solutions based on American principles.

With that in mind, what follows is a quick look at some of the Young Guns candidates we believe are poised to do just that in 2010.

SEAN DUFFY

The American public is waking up to the fact that Washington continues to spend billions of dollars that it doesn't have, raising the national debt to more than $12 trillion. There's no bigger symbol of this out-of-control Washington spending than Wisconsin Rep. David Obey, the chairman of the House spending panel. Obey first set foot in Congress on April 1, 1969, before we landed on the moon and before Woodstock, and his 1960s views of big government spending haven't changed since.

Sean Duffy knows that in order to preserve Wisconsin and America's economic competitiveness, we must address the growing debt crisis that faces our nation. Sean was born and raised in Wisconsin, and currently serves as a prosecutor. Known to a generation of nationwide MTV viewers when he was cast on *The Real World* and later married fellow reality TV castmate Rachel Campos, he is better known locally as the District Attorney of Ashland County, serving in his fourth term and aggressively and responsibly prosecuting crimes with a 90 percent trial success rate. He is also a world-champion lumberjack athlete, carrying on a Wisconsin family tradition.

Like many of the candidates I have met, Sean is very concerned about the out-of-control Washington spending, and how the trillions of dollars of Federal borrowing to pay for bailouts and failed "stimulus" legislation will affect the opportunities and success of his children's generation. And he knows that he can do something to bring fiscal sanity back to Washington, since the architect of the failed "stimulus" bill and bloated spending bills over the past two years is currently his congressman.

Sometimes it takes an entire generation before a fiscally responsible fresh thinker can replace the status quo leader of big-government ideas of the past. Since David Obey first came into Congress in 1969, a generation has passed, and the real world of problems that our country faces cannot be solved by the fiscal philosophies of the 1960s. Sean Duffy provides the people of the 7th District of Wisconsin the opportunity to replace the author of Washington fiscal irresponsibility with a fresh voice who is willing to tackle the out-of-control spending and debt and put our country's finances back on track.

CORY GARDNER

A critical component of *earning* back the majority is fielding quality candidates who can regain the trust of voters in Republican-leaning districts currently represented by Democrats. The GOP must convince voters that we have changed and that our candidates can be trusted.

Colorado's 4th District is an area where we face this challenge and we believe Cory Gardner is the candidate poised to regain that trust and defeat freshman Democratic Rep. Betsy Markey.

Like many of our other candidates, Gardner is a recognized state leader, has deep roots in his state and has the work ethic to succeed. All while supporting the foundational principles of limited government, fiscal responsibility, and accountability.

Gardner is a fifth-generation Coloradan. In 1915 his great granddad, Bill Gardner, opened Gardner and Son's hardware store. The business grew and changed over the years eventually becoming Farmers Implement Company (a farming equipment dealership). The dealership is still owned and operated by the Gardner family today and Cory spends several months each year working side by side with his father and grandfather.

In 2005, Gardner was appointed to represent the 63rd District in the Colorado House of Representatives after a legislative vacancy. He was elected to the seat the following year and chosen by his colleagues shortly after to serve in leadership as minority whip. As a state representative Gardner has proven his leadership abilities and his commitment to innovative ideas that protect the taxpayer and grow the economy.

He has focused much of his time in the Colorado legislature on the critical issues of economic development, health care, and energy. He has won numerous awards including Legislator of the Year from a variety of organizations and the Guardian of the Taxpayer award from the Colorado Union of Taxpayers in 2009.

The race in the 4th District is a critical one. Despite the conservative nature and values of the district, freshman Democrat Betsy Markey has chosen to side with the liberal leadership of Speaker Nancy Pelosi on issue after issue. She voted for the failed stimulus, the job-killing cap-and-trade bill, and the recently passed government takeover of health care. All of these policies will lead to a future of crushing debt and fewer jobs for Coloradans.

In contrast, Gardner is running on a platform of spending restraint and limited government; accountability and transparency; creating jobs and powering the future through private sector growth; real health-care solutions; and a strong national defense.

Cory Gardner represents the commonsense conservatism we need more of in Washington.

CHARLES DJOU

Hawaii isn't the first state that rolls off the tip of the tongue when asked about competitive Republican seats. The state's native son, Barack Obama, won the presidency in 2008 with 72 percent of the state's vote. The two Senate seats have been held by Democrats for more than thirty years, and both House seats have been held by Democrats since statehood, with the exception of a Republican congressman in the first congressional district in Hawaii, who served two terms until 1991. Charles Djou is aiming to make that exception the rule.

Djou was born and raised in Hawaii, and currently serves on the Honolulu City Council. This Army Reserve officer and former floor leader in the Hawaii State House is running for Congress in Hawaii's 1st District.

The reasons why our country is moving in the wrong direction are the same reasons why Charles is running for Congress. He has never voted to raise taxes and wants to make Washington more accountable on spending because, as he says, he knows that every dollar that the government spends comes from hardworking American families. Independent minded, Djou understands how important the public trust is, and has been a leader on major ethics reforms by voting to increase penalties and crack down on corrupt city agencies.

A district whose voters gave 47 percent of the vote to President Bush in 2004, the 1st District wants a representative who reflects its values and represents its interests in Washington. And in Washington, we have seen a Congress move so far to the left and become so disconnected from the people that even the people of Massachusetts said enough, and voted for a Republican to fill the Senate seat vacated after the passing of Ted Kennedy.

In politics, every state and every election are different. But Charles Djou's leadership and ideas to make Hawaii and America stronger have been resonating, and he is eager to help us bring fiscal responsibility and government accountability to Washington.

MARTHA ROBY

Martha Roby, who is running in Alabama's 2nd District, brings a perspective different from those of many candidates who run for Congress. While she too believes that Federal spending and the national debt has grown too large, her desire to bring her conservative ideas and principles to Washington comes from the fact that she wants to help *solve* problems, not *create* problems.

And her service in the Montgomery City Council affords her the experience to listen to the people, identify problems, and reach toward commonsense solutions. She believes in limited government and fiscal responsibility, and has used those principles to fight against five job-killing tax increases and ease the burdens on Montgomery families through local sales tax holidays. As a public servant, she understands the needs in her community and has a track record of focusing solutions on the priorities of the day, rather than partisanship just for the sake of being partisan. Her results-oriented work ethic has been clearly rewarded by the people she serves: she was reelected to the city council in 2007 with an overwhelming 82 percent of the vote.

In a district where Bush received 67 percent of the vote in 2004, and McCain received 63 percent of the vote in 2008, the 2nd District of Alabama currently is represented by freshman Democrat Bobby Bright, who continues to support a Pelosi-led liberal agenda that has added trillions of dollars in debt to current and future generations and created a huge new trillion-dollar government takeover of health care. While Martha has pursued listening to her constituents to solve problems and get results, Bright has allowed the wrong results to win out in Washington, putting our country further in the red.

Alabama needs more representatives willing to fight for their values, and Washington needs more problem solvers willing to stick to their principles and provide common-sense solutions to get our country back on track. The people of the 2nd District of Alabama will find that if they elect Martha Roby, they will have both.

ADAM KINZINGER

Heeding the call to public service at a young age has become a pattern in Illinois (see Aaron Schock), and it has definitely been a hallmark characteristic of Adam Kinzinger.

When Adam was a twenty-year-old sophomore in college, he felt a disconnect between the local government and the people it was supposed to serve, and decided to do something about it. He challenged a twelve-year Democratic incumbent on the McLean County (Illinois) Board and went on to defeat him by promising to listen to the people and fight for commonsense solutions.

Later, after 9/11, Adam heard the call to defend our country and joined the United States Air Force in 2003. Captain Kinzinger served in the Air Force Special Ops, Air Combat Command, Air Mobility Command, and Air National Guard during Operation Enduring Freedom and Operation Iraqi Freedom.

But the call he heard on a Milwaukee street while still serving in the Air National Guard was perhaps the most unexpected. It was the scream of a woman who was bleeding from her throat, being chased by a man with a knife. Unarmed, Kinzinger sprang into action, fought the knife away from the man, and pinned him to the ground along with another person until local police arrived. His act of courage earned him Hero of the Year by the American Red Cross in southeastern Wisconsin.

Now, at the age of thirty-two, after watching what

many Americans have seen in Washington over the past year, Adam is running for the 11th District of Illinois to bring fiscal sanity and accountability back to Washington. He won a five-person Republican primary with almost 64 percent of the vote, and will face Rep. Debbie Halvorson, a freshman Democrat who has supported the job-killing and budget-busting policies of Nancy Pelosi, including the health-care takeover, cap and trade, and the trillion-dollar stimulus bill.

In order to strengthen our economy and preserve the opportunities for the next generation, Adam knows that we need to change the direction of this country, and he is once again ready to answer the call to service and fight for better solutions in Washington for the people of the 11th District.

———— ★ ————

Obviously, there isn't space to talk about all of the great candidates that have been recruited and are running in districts all across the country. The above list is only a glimpse into the quality people who are working hard to change this country and their party for the better. We are excited about supporting them and watching them push toward victory.

A lot has changed in four years since I made the fateful decision to run for Congress in 2006. In many ways it has been more difficult than I might have imagined. The Republican Party has seen some dark times and the challenges our country faces have only grown.

And while the political environment has changed in important ways there is still an epic battle for how this country is to be governed taking place in Washington.

But I am excited about the future because of the people I've discussed here and hundreds like them all over America. The work is hard and we have a long way to go. But we do it because we know it is about more than getting elected. Because, like Stephen Fincher, we know it is about the future for our children and grandchildren. This is about a new commitment to what it means to be an American.

I'm often asked how, if Republicans win back the majority in Congress, we can ensure that we won't violate the people's trust the way the previous Republican majority did. How can we be sure we won't fall back into the high-spending, earmarking culture that was the party's downfall in 2006?

My answer is, through hard work we are re-earning the people's trust. We are making a commitment to America, a commitment in the form of solutions based on our principles.

Should we regain the American people's trust, we will insist that our feet are held to the fire. If given the opportunity to govern, we will deliver on our commitment. If we

don't, I'm confident the American people will send us pack-
ing. That's what democracy is about. We know we don't
have an automatic right to lead. As Ronald Reagan used to
say, America is a nation that has government, not the other
way around. We're ready to be held accountable.

When I walk up those steps in the Capitol Building, I
want to know that I have done all I can to live up to my
ideals and represent the citizens who sent me there. And
when I no longer get goose bumps walking into the People's
House, I'll know it is time to go home.

Appendix A

Members of the House Republican Economic Recovery Working Group

Spencer Bachus (R-AL)
Judy Biggert (R-IL)
Mary Bono Mack (R-CA)
Charles Boustany (R-LA)
Kevin Brady (R-TX)
Dave Camp (R-MI)
John Campbell (R-CA)
Eric Cantor (R-VA)
Shelley Moore Capito (R-WV)
Mike Castle (R-DE)
Ander Crenshaw (R-FL)
David Dreier (R-CA)
Scott Garrett (R-NJ)
Louie Gohmert (R-TX)
Bob Goodlatte (R-VA)
Jeb Hensarling (R-TX)

Darrell Issa (R-CA)
Lynn Jenkins (R-KS)
Bob Latta (R-OH)
Steve LaTourette (R-OH)
Chris Lee (R-NY)
Connie Mack (R-FL)
Kenny Marchant (R-TX)
Kevin McCarthy (R-CA)
Thad McCotter (R-MI)
Jerry Moran (R-KS)
Randy Neugebauer (R-TX)
Erik Paulsen (R-MN)
Mike Pence (R-IN)
Tom Price (R-GA)
Tom Rooney (R-FL)
Peter Roskam (R-IL)
Paul Ryan (R-WI)

Appendix B

Members of the House Republican Young Guns

Steve Austria (R-OH)

Spencer Bachus (R-AL)

Joe Barton (R-TX)

Gus Bilirakis (R-FL)

Marsha Blackburn (R-TN)

John Boehner (R-OH)

Jo Bonner (R-AL)

Mary Bono Mack (R-CA)

Charles Boustany (R-LA)

Kevin Brady (R-TX)

Vern Buchanan (R-FL)

Mike Burgess (R-TX)

Dave Camp (R-MI)

John Campbell (R-CA)

Eric Cantor (R-VA)

Shelley Moore Capito (R-WV)

John Carter (R-TX)

Bill Cassidy (R-LA)

Jason Chaffetz (R-UT)

Howard Coble (R-NC)

Mike Coffman (R-CO)

Tom Cole (R-OK)

Mike Conaway (R-TX)

Ander Crenshaw (R-FL)

John Culberson (R-TX)

Geoff Davis (R-KY)

Charlie Dent (R-PA)

David Dreier (R-CA)

John Duncan (R-TN)

Vern Ehlers (R-MI)

John Fleming (R-LA)

Virginia Foxx (R-NC)

Scott Garrett (R-NJ)

Phil Gingrey (R-GA)

Louie Gohmert (R-TX)

Bob Goodlatte (R-VA)

Kay Granger (R-TX)

Sam Graves (R-MO)
Brett Guthrie (R-KY)
Doc Hastings (R-WA)
Jeb Hensarling (R-TX)
Wally Herger (R-CA)
Duncan Hunter (R-CA)
Darrell Issa (R-CA)
Sam Johnson (R-TX)
Jim Jordan (R-OH)
Jack Kingston (R-GA)
Mark Kirk (R-IL)
John Kline (R-MN)
Tom Latham (R-IA)
Steven LaTourette (R-OH)
Bob Latta (R-OH)
Chris Lee (R-NY)
John Linder (R-GA)
Frank Lucas (R-OK)
Cynthia Lummis (R-WY)
Connie Mack (R-FL)
Kenny Marchant (R-TX)
Kevin McCarthy (R-CA)
Thad McCotter (R-MI)
Patrick McHenry (R-NC)
Buck McKeon (R-CA)
Cathy McMorris Rodgers
  (R-WA)
John Mica (R-FL)
Jeff Miller (R-FL)
Tim Murphy (R-PA)
Randy Neugebauer (R-TX)

Devin Nunes (R-CA)
Pete Olson (R-TX)
Erik Paulsen (R-MN)
Mike Pence (R-IN)
Tom Petri (R-WI)
Ted Poe (R-TX)
Tom Price (R-GA)
Phil Roe (R-TN)
Hal Rogers (R-KY)
Mike Rogers (R-MI)
Tom Rooney (R-FL)
Peter Roskam (R-IL)
Ed Royce (R-CA)
Paul Ryan (R-WI)
Steve Scalise (R-LA)
Aaron Schock (R-IL)
Pete Sessions (R-TX)
John Shadegg (R-AZ)
John Shimkus (R-IL)
Bill Shuster (R-PA)
Adrian Smith (R-NE)
Lamar Smith (R-TX)
Lee Terry (R-NE)
Mac Thornberry (R-TX)
Pat Tiberi (R-OH)
Mike Turner (R-OH)
Fred Upton (R-MI)
Greg Walden (R-OR)
Lynn Westmoreland (R-GA)
Ed Whitfield (R-KY)
Joe Wilson (R-SC)

Acknowledgments

———— ★ ————

ERIC CANTOR

I would like to thank all of my colleagues in the House Republican Conference for their ideas and commitment to America—together we can lead our nation back to greatness. I would also like to thank all my constituents in the 7th District of Virginia who have given me the incredible honor of representing them in Congress. I would also like to thank Mary Matalin, whose guidance and counsel made this book possible. Last, I would not have achieved anything without the love and support of my wife, Diana, and our children, Evan, Jenna, and Michael.

PAUL RYAN

I am grateful for the trust that the people of the first Congressional District of Wisconsin place in me as their representative in Congress. I am also indebted to my wife, Janna, and my children, Liza, Charlie, and Sam. They are my daily reminders of the importance and responsibility to leave a better America for future generations. Thanks!

KEVIN McCARTHY

First and foremost, I would like to thank my wife, Judy, and my children, Connor and Meghan, for their love and support. I am also grateful to the constituents of the 22nd District of California that spans most of Kern and San Luis Obispo Counties and the northeastern portion of Los Angeles County who have entrusted me to represent them in Congress. Finally, I would like to thank my House Republican colleagues and all of our Republican candidates, who continue to fight every day for better solutions to our nation's problems.

Index

Abbas, Mahmoud, 82
accountability: and automobile
  industry, 63; as bipartisan, 152;
  and Cantor's first impressions
  of Washington, 30; and
  Contract with America, 26;
  and elections of 2008, 160; and
  elections of 2009, 66; fostering
  of, 43; lack of congressional,
  152; and need for vision of
  change in Washington, 15;
  "report cards" about, 152; and
  Republican platform, 167; and
  Republican recommitment to
  principles, 135; and Republicans'
  betrayal of principles, 148;
  and Republicans on offense,
  168; and technology, 164; in
  Virginia, 30; and Young Guns
  candidates, 158, 174, 183, 184,
  185, 186, 189; and Young Guns'
  commitment to Americans, 191
Afghanistan, 85
Ahmadinejad, Mahmoud, 79, 80,
  81
AIG, 40
Al-Qaeda, 83
Alabama: Roby 2010 campaign in,
  186–87
alternative strategies, 55, 178

America Speaking Out, 180–81
American Dream, 58
American Energy Act, 62
American exceptionalism, 67
American public: characteristics
  of, 119–20; disconnect
  between Republican leadership
  and, 147; and elections of
  2010, 179; empowerment of,
  180; frustration of, 4, 179;
  ignoring of, 180; legacy of,
  125–26; and need for vision
  of change in Washington, 4,
  12, 15; referendum for, 15; and
  Republican candidates for 2010
  elections, 174; technology as
  means of communicating with,
  164–65; trust of, 12, 70, 148,
  150, 155, 166, 169, 185, 190;
  Young Guns' commitment to,
  177–91
American Recovery and
  Reinvestment Act. See stimulus
  bill
American Red Cross, 188
arrogance, 6, 10, 26, 28, 98–99, 135
automobile industry, 63, 179

Bachmann, Michele, 149
bailouts, 63, 70, 87, 157, 172, 182

Barnes, Fred, 155
Bennett, Bill, 109, 126
Biden, Joseph, 81–82
Biggert, Judy, 46, 172
Bilirakis, Gus, 148–49
bipartisanship: and Clinton
    administration, 28; McCarthy's
    comments about, 146, 152; and
    Obama, 8, 41, 62; and Obama–
    House Republican Working
    Group meeting, 52; and stimulus
    bill, 8, 48–52, 53, 54; and
    strategy of Republicans, 178
blame, 153
Boehner, John, 48, 166, 180
borrowing, 118, 168. *See also* debt/
    deficit
Boyda, Nancy, 158–59, 160
Bridge to Nowhere, 23–24, 25, 37,
    87, 97, 128
Bright, Bobby, 187
Broun, Paul; 149
Brown, Scott, 66, 97
Buchanan, Vern, 149
budget, 26, 63, 71, 74
Budget Committee, U.S. House,
    109, 177
budget reconciliation, 98
bureaucracy, 74–75, 131–32, 135,
    165
Burr, Richard, 166
Bush, George W., 92, 185–86, 187
business: bailout of big, 40;
    building a, 33; and elections
    of 2008, 40; and experience of
    Obama cabinet officials, 34;
    government relationship with big,
    40; government takeover of, 13;
    and health care, 106; pressures
    on congressmen from, 128;
    regulation of, 128; and stimulus
    bill, 54–55. *See also* corporations;
    small business
Byrd family, 32

cabinet, Obama: prior experience of
    members of, 34–35

Cairo, Egypt: Obama speech in, 83
California; and McCarthy's
    elections as representative from,
    142, 145–46
California State Assembly;
    McCarthy in, 146, 163
Camp, Dave, 46, 49
Campbell, John, 152
Campos, Rachel, 181
candidates, Young Guns:
    benchmarks for, 171; for elections
    of 2010, 170–75, 181–89; and
    formation of Young Guns,
    156–57; Young Guns'
    commitment to, 156
Cantor, Eddie, 31, 32–33
Cantor, Eric: differences and
    commonalities among Ryan,
    McCarthy and, 19–20; first
    impressions of Washington of,
    29–30; and need for vision of
    change in Washington, 3–16;
    as new-generation Republican
    leader, 155; personal and
    professional background of,
    30–31, 33; as Republican whip,
    40–41, 177; self-image of, 33;
    as small-businessman, 33, 46;
    threats against, 86–87; and
    Young Guns organization, 156.
    See also Young Guns; *specific topic*
Cantor, Evan, 40
Cantor, Jenna, 40
Cantor, Michael, 40
cap-and-trade bill, 59, 60–61, 87,
    172, 178, 184, 189
Capito, Shelley Moore, 46
Capitol Building, U.S.: McCarthy's
    feelings about, 141–42, 191
careerism, 5, 35
Chaffetz, Jason, 172
change: Cantor's comments about,
    20–21, 23, 27, 62, 66, 68;
    Contract with America as spirit
    of, 27; and elections of 2008,
    23, 130, 133; enduring, 14;
    and formation of Young Guns,

156–57; leadership for, 21;
McCarthy's comments about,
142, 150, 156–57, 162, 167,
172, 174, 175, 189–90; need
for, 3–16, 66, 68; Obama as
hope for, 62, 66; in political
environment since 2006, 189–90;
progressive vision of, 133; and
remaking of Republican Party,
162; in Republican Party, 167;
Republican vision of, 133–34;
rhetoric of, 133; Ryan's comments
about, 130, 133–34, 135; source
of, 20–21; and Young Guns
candidates for 2010 elections,
172, 174, 175
China, 118, 136, 179
choice: and future of America,
111–23; need for, 123; rhetoric
of, 8; and Ryan's Roadmap for
America, 138
Christie, Chris, 66
Chrysler Corporation, 63
Churchill, Winston, 43
"citizen legislators," 27
civil rights movement, 32
Clinton, Bill, 27, 126
Clinton, Hillary, 80, 82
CNN: survey by, 22
Coburn, Tom, 27
Coelho, Tony, 26
Cole, Tom, 170
Collins, Jim, 152
Collins, Susan, 55
Colorado: Gardner 2010 campaign
in, 183–84
Committee for Honest
Government, Illinois, 162
Committee on House
Administration, 165
community organizers: as Obama
advisers, 10
compassion, 120, 121
competition, 43, 104, 107, 110, 152
Congress, U.S.: communication
between constituents and
members of, 165; health-care

plan for members of, 137;
pressures on members of, 127–
28; retirement plan for members
of, 137; technology uses in,
163–67; understanding of small
business in, 35. *See also* House
of Representatives, U.S Senate,
specific member
Congressional Budget Office
(CBO), 45, 51, 100, 102, 117,
118, 122, 136
consent of the people, 94, 99, 123
conservatives, 33, 37, 58–59, 168,
178, 184, 186
Constitution, U.S., 9, 94, 127, 131,
133, 134–35
Contract with America, 5, 26–27,
28
"Cornhusker Kickback," 96
corporations, 40, 70, 72, 77, 87,
137, 157. *See also* business
corruption, 5, 15, 26, 29, 94, 97,
128, 147, 178, 185
crisis: Democrats as exploiting,
106; Emanuel's views about, 62,
95; and entitlements, 115–16;
as excuse for health-care reform,
95; and need for change in
Washington, 21;
"phony," 22. *See also specific crisis*
cronyism, 15, 75, 87

Davis, Geoff, 172
debt/deficit: and alternative strategy
of Republicans, 178; Americans'
concern about, 64–65; and
commitment of Young Guns,
179; and differences in American
politics today, 111; drivers of,
116; and elections of 2008, 159;
and entitlements, 116; and health
care, 64, 100, 102–3; interest
on, 64; and need for change, 4,
11, 21; Obama's comment about,
100; projected, 122; Republicans'
commitment to lowering, 72; as
Republicans' No. 1 priority, 45;

debt/deficit *(cont.)*
  size of, 11; and stimulus bill, 56,
  57; and taxes, 72; and tipping
  point, 58, 110; and up-or-down
  vote, 98; and Washington as part
  of problem, 126; and Young Guns
  candidates for 2010 elections,
  172, 181, 182, 186, 187
Declaration of Independence, 127,
  131, 134
"deem and pass," 98, 99
Democrats: backroom deals/
  scandals of, 26, 178; failure of,
  178–79; as focusing on American
  flaws, 67; mandate for, 7; one-
  party rule by, 21, 25–26, 63; as
  party of "no," 147; as political
  machine, 26, 32; procedural
  tricks of, 156; vulnerable, 156,
  168, 169. *See also specific person
  or topic*
demographics, 16
dependency, 42, 110, 111, 114–15,
  120, 132
dissent, 36, 86–87
Djou, Charles, 185–86
"Dollars for a Classroom" bill
  (Pitts), 74
domestic policy: basic test for, 70
Doolittle, James "Jimmy," 168–69
Dowd, Maureen, 56
Duffy, Sean, 181–82
Dukakis, Michael, 126

earmarks, 3–4, 5, 29, 74, 128, 148,
  153, 167
economic freedom, 20, 33, 37, 79
economy: and choices for America's
  future, 113; comparison of
  European and American, 43; and
  Democrats' vision of America,
  122; dissatisfaction with, 133;
  and elections of 2008, 40, 159;
  and experience of Obama cabinet
  members, 34; free fall of, 118–19;
  global, 110; and Keynesian
  economics, 46, 47, 50; and need

for vision of change, 11; Obama
  as inheriting, 153; "report cards"
  about, 152; and Republican
  alternative job plan, 71–72;
  and Republican platform, 167;
  as Republicans' No. 1 priority,
  45; and Republicans' return to
  founding principles, 129; and
  Ryan's Roadmap for America,
  137; and stimulus bill, 54; and
  tipping point, 110, 121, 122; and
  Washington Way, 95; in Western
  Europe, 42; and Young Guns
  candidates for 2010 elections,
  173, 184; and Young Guns'
  commitment to America, 177
education, 14–15, 73–74, 133
Education, U.S. Department of, 14
elections of 1994, 28
elections of 2004, 185, 187
elections of 2006, 40, 146–48,
  150, 158
elections of 2008, 23, 40, 62, 130,
  133, 157, 167–68, 170, 187
elections of 2010, 12, 170–75, 179,
  181–89
elections of 2012, 12
elections, special, 65–66, 96, 97,
  178, 179, 186
Emanuel, Rahm, 50, 62, 95
employers: health-care insurance
  from, 104
Empower America, 109
energy, 61–62, 70, 73, 113, 167,
  179, 184. *See also* cap-and-trade
  bill
Energy and Commerce Committee,
  U.S. House of Representatives,
  35
entitlements: Americans' historic
  views about, 119–20; bankruptcy
  of, 121; and debt/deficit, 116;
  and Democrats mandate for far-
  left agenda, 62; and Democrats'
  views of America, 68; expansion
  of, 121, 122; need for reform
  of, 120–21, 122; and need for

vision of change, 11, 13, 16;
and Republican recommitment
to principles, 134; and Ryan's
Roadmap for America, 93, 136;
spending on, 115–16; and taxes,
72; and tipping point, 115–16,
135; unfunded liability of, 117;
in Western Europe, 42. *See also*
Medicaid; Medicare; Social
Security
entrepreneurship, 12, 29, 30, 43,
46, 110, 120, 121, 134, 144
environment. *See* cap-and-trade
bill; energy
equality, 79, 129, 134
Europe: dependency in, 114–15; as
model for America, 42–43, 63;
productivity in, 115; taxes in,
115; unemployment in, 115; as
welfare state, 6, 42–43, 63, 111,
115, 130, 132, 133
European Union, 111, 122

Facebook, 48, 165
Fallin, Mary, 149
family values, 20, 28, 33, 37, 112
Fannie Mae, 59
Fatah party, 82–83
Federal Bureau of Investigation
(FBI), 86
financial/fiscal crisis, 136, 138. *See
also* recession
financial institutions, 133, 179
Financial Services Committee, U.S.
House, 129
Fincher, Stephen, 173–74, 183, 190
fiscal policies: and America as rock
of stability, 43; and elections
of 2008, 159–60; McCarthy's
early thoughts about, 142–43;
and Republican platform, 167;
and Republicans as losing their
way, 25; and Ryan's Roadmap for
America, 138; and Young Guns
candidates, 158, 174, 182, 183,
186, 189
Florida: "Gator Aid" for, 96

force: and foreign relations, 81
foreign policy, 70, 77–86
Frank, Barney, 59, 129
Franking Commission, U.S. House,
165
Freddie Mac, 59
free enterprise, 105, 119, 123, 179
free market, 10, 12, 28, 57, 69, 126,
129
freedom: America as greatest
experiment in, 108; and
Cantor's vision of America, 31;
individual, 20, 36; and need for
vision of change, 11, 13; and
new Republican leadership, 69;
and pressures on congressmen,
128; and principles, 111;
and Republican vision of
America, 133; and Republicans'
reconnection with founding
principles, 129, 134; rhetoric of,
8. *See also type of freedom*
freedom of speech, 79
freedom to worship, 79
Friedman, Milton, 103

Gard, John, 155–56
Gardner, Cory, 183–84
"Gator Aid," 96
General Motors Corporation, 63
Gingrich Revolution, 25
Gore, Al, 126
government: and alternative strategy
of Republicans, 178; and America
as land of promise, 43; and
anxiety about future of America,
65; big, 42, 43, 63–64, 65, 75,
106, 107, 132, 178; centralization
of, 131–32; and choices for
America's future, 113; CNN
survey about, 22; control by, 172;
Democrats' views about, 20; and
dependency agenda, 42; and
differences in American politics
today, 111; dissatisfaction with,
133; Frank's comment about,
129; goal/purpose of, 108, 134;

government (*cont.*)
  growth/expansion of, 22, 42, 107, 111, 129, 148, 150; intrusion by, 20, 25, 134; jobs in, 15; and need for change, 11–12, 13, 68–69; Obama's views about, 63; as obstacle, 143; progressives' views about, 111, 132; Reagan's comment about, 113; redefinition of relationship between Americans and, 106; and Republican platform, 167; Republican views about, 20; and Republicans' alternative jobs plan, 71; and Republicans in early 2000s, 150; and Republicans' reconnection with founding principles, 134; and Ryan's Roadmap for America, 138; size of, 11–12, 20, 41; smarter, 41, 63, 167; spending as perpetuating big, 75; takeovers by, 13, 87, 100–102, 111, 132, 184, 187, 189; technology use in, 164–65; and tipping point, 135; in Western Europe, 42; and Young Guns candidates, 172. *See also* limited government; *specific topic*
Guantánamo Bay, 70, 83, 84

Halvorson, Debbie, 189
Hamas, 84
Hart, Gary, 4–5
Hastert, Denny, 78
Hawaii: Djou 2010 campaign in, 185–86; Obama 2008 vote in, 185
Health and Human Services, U.S. Department of, 101, 102
health care: and alternative strategy of Republicans, 178; antimarket character of, 68; backroom deals/corruption concerning, 76, 94, 96–97; and big government, 63–64, 106, 107; as broken system, 63–64; and choices for America's future, 112–13; and commitment of Young Guns,

179; and competition, 104, 107; as completing progressive agenda, 9; costs of, 64, 76, 77, 100, 102, 103, 105, 106, 107, 110, 116, 118, 136; debate about, 86–87, 93–94, 104, 105–6; and debt/deficit, 64, 100, 102–3; Democrats' work on, 70; and dependency, 42; and elections of 2009, 96; employer, 104; exclusion of Republicans from, 99; financial crisis as excuse for, 95; and insurers crossing state lines, 105, 107; and jobs, 75; and media, 86; for members of Congress, 137; as missed opportunity, 106–7; and need for vision of change, 9, 10, 13; 1960s program for, 120; and Obama at House Republican retreat, 91; opposition to, 75, 86–87, 95–96, 99, 106; passage of, 98–99; and pre-existing conditions, 101, 106; and principles, 105; problems with, 100–103; and progressive vision, 132; and promises of Democrats, 68; and "public option," 100; and quality of care, 75; and regulation, 104–5; repeal of, 76, 77; Republican proposal for, 75–77, 104–6; and size of government, 63–64; and spending, 64; and stimulus bill, 102; takeover of, 13, 87, 100–102, 111, 132, 184, 187, 189; and taxes, 75, 76, 77, 104–5, 107; and technology, 104–5; and tipping point, 110, 132; universal, 112, 136; votes for, 97, 106; and Washington Way, 96–98, 106; and winning at any cost, 100; writing of, 76, 96; and Young Guns candidates for 2010 elections, 172, 184, 187, 189. *See also* Medicare
Heller, Dean, 149
Hensarling, Jeb, 46

Hezbollah, 84
home-buyers credit, 49
hope, 22–23, 31, 41, 62, 69, 172
House banking scandal, 26
House of Representatives, U.S.:
"deem and pass" in, 98, 99;
Democratic control of, 148, 157;
and legislative agenda, 45; 1994
Republican class in, 27–28;
procedures of, 156; "report card"
for, 151–52, 153; Republican
losses in, 40; Republican
solidarity in, 157; Republicans
as minority in, 44; Resident
Commissioners of, 44; 2006
Republican class in, 148–49, 151;
yearly retreat of Republicans in,
91–92
House Republican Economic
Recovery Working Group, 47–52
housing, 59, 60, 74, 87, 113, 153,
158, 178
Hurricane Katrina, 24

ideology, 62, 69, 108, 111, 130
Illinois: Kinzinger 2010 campaign
in, 188–89; Schock election in,
161–63, 188
inauguration, Obama's, 39, 43–44,
66
incentives, 61, 119, 136, 137
Independents, 22, 66, 133, 148
inflation, 118
initiative, 110, 132, 134
innovation, 61, 120, 132, 134, 143,
167, 179
interest rates, 118
internships, unpaid, 144–45
Iran, 79–81, 83–84
Iraq, 56, 85, 160, 188
Israel, 79, 81–84

Japan, 136
Jenkins, Lynn, 158–60
Jerusalem, 82
jobs: and basic test for domestic
policy, 70; and commitment
of Young Guns, 180; and
dependency agenda, 42;
and elections of 2008, 40,
158; and elections of 2009,
66; and energy issues, 61, 73;
and entrepreneurship, 144;
in government, 15; "green,"
73; and health care, 75; and
Keynesian economics, 46;
lack of Democratic activity
about, 71; manufacturing, 15;
and need for vision of change,
12, 15; and new generation of
Republican leadership, 71; and
Obama at House Republican
retreat, 91; in private sector,
20; "report cards" about, 153;
Republican alternative plans
for, 46, 48, 50, 51, 71–72; and
Republican solidarity, 179; as
Republicans' No. 1 priority, 45;
and Republicans on offensive,
168; and Ryan's Roadmap for
America, 137; small business
as source of, 47; and source of
change in Washington, 20;
and stimulus bill, 46, 48, 50,
51, 54, 57, 71, 152; and taxes,
71, 72; and tipping point, 121;
Washington as disconnected
from creating and maintaining,
34; and Washington Way, 95;
and Young Guns candidates in
2010 elections, 184, 186–87. *See
also* unemployment
Joint Economic Committee, U.S.
House-Senate, 115
Jordan, 84
Jordan, Jim, 149, 172
J.P. Morgan, 34

Kansas: Jenkins election in, 158–60
Kemp, Jack, 109, 126
Kennedy, Edward "Ted," 97, 186
Keynesian economics, 46, 47, 50
Kinzinger, Adam, 188–89
Krohn, Cyrus, 166

LaHood, Ray, 162
Lamborn, Doug, 148–49
Latta, Bob, 149
leadership: McCarthy's comments about, 152; need for new, 88; and need for vision of change, 15; new generation of Republican, 67–88, 179–80; and Republican control in Washington, 21
Lee, Chris, 46
legislative agenda, 28–29, 44–45
Levi, Primo, 79
Levin, Yuval, 103
liberals, 130–31, 173
liberty, 10, 37, 69, 105, 123, 129, 131, 134
Limbaugh, Rush, 52
limited government: compared with governments in Europe, 42; and Constitution, 131; and elections of 2008, 160; and elections of 2009, 65, 96; and health care, 105; McCarthy's early beliefs in, 143; and new generation of leaders, 69; Republican belief in, 20, 28; Republican loyalty to, 129; and Republicans' losing way, 128; and Ryan's campaign for House, 126; and tipping point, 114; in Virginia, 32; and Young Guns candidates, 158, 183, 184, 186
Lincoln, Abraham, 21, 67
Los Angeles Times, 71
"Louisiana Purchase," 76, 96

Madia, Ashwin, 160–61
Madison, James, 29
Madoff, Bernie, 40
mandates, 71, 179
manufacturing jobs, 15
Markey, Betsy, 183, 184
Massachusetts: special election of 2010 in, 65–66, 97, 178, 179, 186
McCain, John, 187
McCarthy, Jeremiah, 145

McCarthy, Kevin: Capitol Building feelings of, 141–42, 191; as chief recruiter for elections of 2010, 171–75; differences and commonalities among Cantor, McCarthy and, 19–20; first experience in public service of, 144–45; idealism of, 145; as lottery winner, 143; as member of Republican House freshman class of 2006, 148–49; and need for vision of change, 3–16; personal and professional background of, 142–46; as Republican Deputy Whip, 177; as small-businessman, 143–44; travels of, 146–47, 155, 163, 172–73; 2006 campaign of, 146–48, 190. *See also* Young Guns; *specific topic*
McDonnell, Bob, 66
media, 56, 86, 87, 166
Medicaid, 96, 115, 116, 120, 136, 137
Medicare, 92, 102, 103, 115, 116, 117, 120, 136–37
Michel, Bob, 149
Middle East, 81, 83–84. *See also specific nation*
Minnesota: Paulsen election in, 160–61
minorities, 36
mortgage crisis, 59–60, 153
Mughrabi, Dalal, 82–83
Myrick, Sue, 27

Napolitano, Janet, 166
National Republican Congressional Committee (NRCC), 169, 170–71
national security, 61, 70, 80, 83, 84, 180, 184. *See also* terrorism
Nebraska: "Cornhusker Kickback" for, 96
Netanyahu, Benjamin, 82
New Deal, 9
New Jersey: elections of 2009 in, 65–66, 96, 178, 179

New York City: terrorism in, 85
New York Times, 20, 56, 82–83
"no," 45, 52, 54, 56, 147
North Korea, 83
"nuclear option," 98
nuclear weapons, 79–80, 83, 84

Obama, Barack: advisers to, 10;
approval ratings of, 53–54; and
bipartisanship, 8, 41, 62; Cairo
speech of, 83; and cap-and-trade
bill, 61; as centrist, 7, 130; and
change, 130; and debt, 100;
election comment of, 52; and
elections of 2008, 167–68; as far-
left, 7–8; and health care, 100;
and hope for change, 62, 66;
and House Republican retreat,
91–92; House Republican
Working Group meeting with,
48–52; Illinois award for, 162;
inauguration of, 39, 43–44,
66; and Iraq War, 85; lack
of focus on spending of, 135;
partisanship of, 52; popularity
of, 58; promise to change
Washington ways of, 41; and size
of government, 63; and stimulus
bill, 8, 56
Obamacare. *See* health care
Obey, David, 51, 181, 182
oil: dependence on foreign, 73
Olmert, Ehud, 78
Olson, Pete, 172
one-party rule, 21, 25–26, 63
opportunity: and America as land
of promise, 43; and American
Dream, 58; and American
exceptionalism, 67; and anxiety
about future of America, 65;
Cantor's belief in, 31, 32;
and Cantor's childhood and
youth, 33; and Cantor's vision
of America, 36; and choices
for America's future, 113; and
Democrats' views of America,
68, 69; to direct change to make

America great, 133–34; and
elections of 2009, 66; equal, 9,
10; and goal of government, 108;
health-care reform as missed,
106–7; McCarthy's early beliefs
in, 143; and need for vision of
change in Washington, 8, 9,
10, 12, 16; and new Republican
leadership, 69; and pressures
on congressmen, 128; and
principles, 111; and rebuilding
of Republican Party, 180; and
Republicans' need for return to
founding principles, 129; rhetoric
of, 8; right to, 127; and source
of change in Washington, 20;
and tipping point, 110; and
Young Guns candidates for 2010
elections, 182
Orszag, Peter, 50, 92

Palestinians, 82–83, 84
Parade magazine: "Bridge to
Nowhere" story in, 23, 24, 25
partisanship, 52, 110, 174, 177–78,
187
party of "no," 45, 52, 56, 147
paternalism, 68–69, 98–99, 108,
110, 111, 130, 138
Patient's Choice Act, 104–5
Paulsen, Erik, 160–61
Pelosi, Nancy: and cap-and-trade
bill, 61; and health-care reform,
96, 98, 99; liberalism of, 35;
and need for vision of change in
Washington, 4, 8; overreaching
by, 172; and Republicans
on offensive, 168, 169; and
stimulus bill, 8, 52–53, 54; and
vulnerable Democrats, 169; and
Young Guns candidates for 2010
elections, 172, 184, 187, 189
Pitts, Joe, 14, 74
Platform Committee, Democratic,
166
Platform Committee, Republican,
166–67

political machines, 26, 28, 29, 32, 87
politicians: as "citizen legislators,"
    27; professional, 27, 35
politics: of fear, 68; importance of,
    178; as "local," 147; McCarthy's
    views about, 151; principles
    as major difference in today's,
    110–11
post office scandal, 26
Preventive Services Task Force,
    U.S., 101–2
Price, Tom, 46, 171–72
prices, consumer, 118
principles: and Cantor's
    identification with Republican
    Party, 31; center-right, 28;
    and commonalities among
    Cantor, McCarthy, and Ryan,
    20; conservative, 37, 153;
    core, 70; and differences
    in American politics today,
    110–11; and elections of 2009,
    65–66; and foreign relations,
    79; and health care, 105; and
    listening to voters, 166; nation's
    founding, 6, 7, 37, 105, 123,
    133; need for new commitment
    to, 135; and need for vision
    of change, 6, 7, 13, 15; and
    new generation of Republican
    leadership, 70; and opposition
    to Democratic programs, 69;
    parties' abandonment of, 20;
    of Republican Party, 28, 33,
    37; and Republican vision of
    change, 133–34; Republicans'
    abandonment of their, 129;
    Republicans as betraying
    their, 148; and Republicans as
    losing their way, 25, 28–29;
    Republicans' need to reconnect
    with, 21, 134; Republicans'
    rededication to founding, 123;
    and special interests, 20; and
    Young Guns candidates in 2010
    elections, 186; and Young Guns'
    commitment to Americans, 190

private sector, 20, 34, 35, 43, 47, 51,
    71, 118, 164, 184
productivity, 113, 115, 118, 164
progressives, 9, 98, 99, 111, 112,
    121, 129–33

race, 32, 87
Ramstad, Jim, 160, 161
Rangel, Charlie, 152
Reagan Revolution, 24
Reagan, Ronald, 21, 67, 102, 113,
    142, 191
recession, 136, 157
reconciliation bill, 94
referendum, 15
regulation, 43, 71–72, 104–5, 121,
    128, 167
Reid, Harry, 52–53, 54, 96
"report card," 151–52, 153
Republican Economic Recovery
    Working Group, U.S. House,
    47, 49
Republican National Convention
    (2008), 166–67
Republicans: alternative strategy
    of, 178; Americans' reconnection
    with, 156; as betraying their
    principles, 148; change in, 167;
    confidence of, 57–58, 169; control
    by, 21; corruption/scandals of, 5,
    128, 147, 150; credibility of, 58;
    disconnect between American
    people and leadership of, 147;
    failures of, 148; generational
    change in, 162; lack of trust in,
    25; leadership for, 28, 67–88,
    147, 175, 179–80; as losing their
    way, 20, 23–30, 37, 150; myth
    of, 31; need for refocusing of, 12;
    need to change image of, 150; as
    needing to remake the party, 153;
    as obstructionists, 178; as party
    of innovation, 167; performance
    reports for, 24; as political
    machine, 5, 28; principles
    of, 21, 28, 33, 37, 123, 134;
    rebuilding of, 150–53; reputation

of, 150; solidarity among, 177; strengthening of, 57–59; vision of change of, 133–34; Young Guns as not repeating mistakes of earlier, 158. *See also* Young Guns

Resident Commissioners, House, 44

retirement, 42, 112, 120, 137

rhetoric, 8, 87, 133

rights, 108, 127, 131, 134. *See also specific right*

"A Roadmap for America's Future" (Ryan), 92–93, 106, 136–38

Roby, Martha, 186–87

Rodgers, Cathy McMorris, 172

Romney, Mitt, 47

Ros-Lehtinen, Ileana, 78

Roskam, Peter, 45–46, 149, 180

Rostenkowski, Dan, 26

Rules Committee, U.S. House, 44, 164

Russia, 83

Ryan, Paul: as Budget Committee member, 109, 177; differences and commonalities among Cantor, McCarthy and, 19–20; idealism of, 127; and need for vision of change, 3–16; as new-generation Republican leader, 155; personal and professional background of, 125–27; and Young Guns organization, 156. *See also* Young Guns; *specific topic*

Ryun, Jim, 158–59

safety net, 105, 112–13, 120, 138

salaries, 14

San Francisco Chronicle, 61

Saudi Arabia, 84

Scalise, Steve, 149

Schock, Aaron, 161–63, 188

Schultz, Debbie Wasserman, 78

Senate, U.S., 45, 98, 157

senior citizens, 68, 92

September 11, 2001, 86

Sessions, Pete, 170, 171

Shadegg, John, 27

Shuster, Bill, 172

small business: and Cantor as small-businessman, 33; and cap-and-trade bill, 60; and health care, 76, 104; and jobs, 47, 71, 72; and McCarthy as small-businessman, 143–44; motivation of, 43; and need for change, 68; Obama administration lack of understanding of, 35; Obama team as disconnected from concerns of, 50–51; and Republican alternative job plan, 71, 72; and Republican alternative stimulus bill, 46, 47, 48, 49, 50–51; as source of innovation, 47; and spending by Obama administration, 63; and tipping point, 110

Smith, Adrian, 149

Snow, Olympia, 55

social networks, 165

Social Security, 92, 112, 115, 116, 117, 120, 136, 137

special interests, 20, 30, 40, 51, 54, 74–75, 127–28

Specter, Arlen, 55

spending: and alternative strategy of Republicans, 178; and basic test for domestic policy, 70; and budget reconciliation, 98; and commitment of Young Guns, 179; comparison of European and American, 43; crisis in, 21; Democrats' plans for, 70; and Democrats' vision of America, 68, 122; and differences in American politics today, 111; discretionary, 72; and elections of 2008, 159; and failures of Republicans, 148; and family as analogy for choice about America's future, 112; and federal–state relations, 74; and health care, 64; in industrialized countries, 115; and Keynesian economics, 46; and meaningful reform, 41;

spending (cont.)
and need for vision of change, 13;
Obama's lack of focus on, 135; as
perpetuating big government, 75;
and pressures on congressmen,
127–28, 129; "report cards"
about, 152, 153; and Republican
alternative stimulus bill, 46, 47;
Republican views about, 20; and
Republicans as losing their way,
25; by Republicans in early 2000s,
150; and Republicans on offensive,
168; and Ryan's Roadmap
for America, 136; and size of
government, 63; and stimulus bill,
54, 56; and taxes, 72; and tipping
point, 58, 109–10, 122, 135; and
2009 budget, 63; in Virginia, 30;
and Young Guns candidates for
2010 elections, 172, 181, 182, 184,
185, 186
standard of living, 118–19, 126
states, 13
stimulus bill: and alternative
strategy of Republicans, 178;
and bipartisanship, 8, 48–52,
53, 54; business groups support
of, 54; and deficit, 56; and
health care, 102; and jobs, 54,
57, 71, 152; and Keynesian
economics, 47; and media, 56;
and need for vision of change,
8; and new generation of
Republican leadership, 71; and
Obama approval ratings, 53–54;
opposition to, 54–55, 56–57;
passage of, 55, 57–58; Pelosi-Reid
creation of, 52–53, 54; as pork-
laden, 54; and progressive vision,
132; Republican alternative to,
8, 45–46, 48–52, 54, 55–56, 59,
71, 178; Republican reactions
to, 57–59; Republican solidarity
against, 179; and Republicans
on offensive, 168; and size of
government, 63; as turning point
for Obama administration, 56;

and Young Guns candidates for
2010 elections, 182, 184, 189
stock market, 118
Summers, Larry, 50
Supreme Court, U.S., 131

Taliban, 85
Tanner, John, 173–74
TARP. *See* stimulus bill
tax credits, 60, 104–5
Tax Foundation, 114
taxes: and budget reconciliation,
98; corporation, 72, 137; and
deficit, 72; and Democrats' views
of America, 68; and education,
74; and elections of 2008, 159;
energy, 61, 70; and entitlements,
72; in Europe, 42, 115; as
fostering capital markets, 43; and
health care, 75, 76, 77, 104, 107;
and income tax rates, 117–18;
in industrialized countries, 115;
and jobs, 71, 72; lowering of,
121; payroll, 118; and private
sector, 71; and progressive vision,
132; and Republican alternative
plans, 49, 50, 51, 60, 71, 72; and
Republican platform, 167; and
Republicans on offensive, 168;
and Ryan's Roadmap for America,
92, 137; and Social Security, 117;
and stimulus bill, 49, 50, 51; and
tipping point, 114, 117–18; value-
added, 72; in Virginia, 32; and
Young Guns candidates for 2010
elections, 172, 185, 186–87
Tea Party, 172
technology, 104–5, 163–67
Tel Aviv, Israel: terrorist attack in, 78
Tennessee: Fincher 2010 campaign
in, 173–74, 183
terrorism, 78, 80, 83–85, 86
Thomas, Bill, 144–45, 146
Thornberry, Mac, 27
Time magazine, 54
Times Square bomber, 85
tipping point, 109–10, 114, 132, 134

Tocqueville, Alexis de, 132–33
tolerance, 31, 36
town hall meetings, 4, 75, 95, 164, 166, 172, 180
transparency, 26, 98, 104–5, 107, 148, 164, 180, 184
transportation, 14, 74
trial lawyers, 10, 77, 105
Truman, Harry S., 67
trust, 70, 148, 150, 155, 166, 169, 185, 190
Twitter, 165
"underwear bomber," 85
unemployment: and cap-and-trade bill, 61; and choices for America's future, 112; comparison of European and American, 43; in Europe, 42, 115; and experience of Obama cabinet members, 45; and health care, 104; in industrialized countries, 115; and progressive vision, 132; "report cards" about, 152; as Republicans' No. 1 priority, 45; and stimulus bill, 49, 57; and tipping point, 110, 135; and Young Guns candidates for 2010 elections, 173. *See also* jobs
Union of Taxpayers, Colorado, 184
unions, 10, 63, 77, 145
United Nations, 80
"up or down vote," 98

value-added taxes, 72
Van Hollen, Chris, 56–57
Virginia: accountability in, 30; Democratic control of, 32; education in, 73; elections of 2009 in, 65–66, 96, 178, 179; limited government in, 32; racial integration in, 32; spending in, 30; tax culture in, 32
Volcker, Paul, 72

Walsh, Brian, 172
Washington, D.C.: Cantor's first impressions of, 29–30;

as insulating, 25; new way in, 94–95; Obama's promise to change ways of, 41; as part of problem, 126; protocol in, 48
Washington Way, 93–98, 106, 127–28
Waxman, Henry, 35
Ways and Means Committee, U.S. House, 35, 49
wealth, 10, 46, 61
The Weekly Standard, 155
welfare: Americans' historical views about, 119–20; Clinton reform of, 27–28; and compassion, 121; and Europe as welfare state, 6, 42–43, 63, 111, 115, 130, 132, 133; and need for vision of change, 6; and Ryan's Roadmap for America, 138
Westmoreland, Lynn, 171–72
WhipCast, 105, 165
Whitman, Meg, 47
Will, George, 42
Wilson, Woodrow, 131
winning; focus on, 28
Wisconsin: Duffy campaign in, 181–82; and Ryan, 122–23, 126–27
Wittman, Rob, 149, 172
women: equal rights for, 79
Wright, Jim, 26

Young Guns: Barnes' christening of, 155; and benchmarks for candidates, 171; and candidates for 2010 elections, 181–89; commitment to Americans by, 177–91; commitment to candidates by, 156; and elections of 2008, 157–63; goals of, 156–57; House Republican colleagues join, 157; on offensive, 169–75; organization of, 156; successes of, 157–63, 170; website for, 171
YouTube, 48, 96, 165